C000269949

CATTLE, CORN & CRAWFISH
900 YEARS OF CHICHESTER'S MARKETS

A view of East Street, Chichester, looking west from Eastgate Square, on 26 April 1871, the last day of the beast market in the streets. This view provides an excellent impression of the chaos the beast market caused before it was transferred to the new cattle market in Market Road. Posts and chains have been provided to keep the animals off the pavement, but the wandering cattle and the resultant ordure would have made crossing the street a somewhat unsavoury task. In the middle distance can be seen the portico of the Corn Exchange.

CATTLE, CORN & CRAWFISH
900 YEARS OF CHICHESTER'S MARKETS

Alan H.J. Green

Phillimore

2011
Published by
PHILLIMORE & CO. LTD
Andover, Hampshire, England

www.phillimore.co.uk

© Alan H.J. Green, 2011
All rights reserved

ISBN 978-1-86077-699-1

Printed and bound in Malta
by Gutenberg Press

Manufacturing managed by
Jellyfish Solutions Ltd

Contents

List of Illustrations

Frontispiece: View of East Street from Eastgate Square, 1871, the last day of the old beast market.

Acknowledgements

A work of this size and nature can only be produced with the assistance of others and I owe thanks to a large number of people in this respect. Writing acknowledgements carries with it a great risk of omitting someone, so if I am found to have committed this sin I crave pardon – it was certainly not deliberate but the result of ever-increasing senior moments.

I begin with the staff of West Sussex Record Office (WSRO) where the bulk of the research was undertaken. The WSRO staff are always so helpful and patient and certainly deserve the award of their four gold stars; tracking down some of the Corn Exchange material contained within the Raper Uncatalogued collection was not an easy task.

The second repository of information was Chichester District Museum, where there is an enviable collection of market-related artefacts, and the museum staff kindly granted me access to these. I would particularly thank Simon Kitchen for sharing his previous researches into the Cattle Market and Terry Carlysle and Sam Fieldhouse who sought out and scanned photographs in the museum's collection for inclusion in this work, which are reproduced by kind permission.

My old school-friend Dr David Pilbeam of Leeds University kindly read through Chapter One on the agriculture of Chichester and supplied helpful comments and additional information. David Sadler and Pat Combes, descendants of founders of the Corn Exchange and successors in their family firms, very kindly let me raid their archives for material and photographs relating to the Corn Exchange and its resurgence after the collapse of the Corn Exchange Company.

On the Cattle Market front the staff of Stride & Son were similarly very helpful in providing information about the firm's long involvement in the Cattle Market. Nick Stride kindly loaned me a copy of the Stride family history while Derek Bowerman and Imogen Stuart shared their memories and granted me access to the photographs in the company archives; I am particularly indebted to Imogen for permitting me to include in the *Envoi* her sonnet written to mark the 10th anniversary of the closure of the Cattle Market. Verity Waite of John Wiley and Sons kindly loaned me Corn Exchange photographs from the Wiley archive and granted me permission to publish them. A copy of an important part of the legislation regarding the Market House was missing from both WSRO and the City Council archive and I am grateful to Rodney Duggua, the town clerk, who managed to obtain a copy from the House of Lords library. The Royal Institute of British Architects supplied a copy of Nash's drawing of the Market House and kindly granted permission for it to be published here, and I am grateful to the Dean and Chapter of Chichester Cathedral, who kindly granted me access to the cathedral library in order to copy the only known photograph of the interior of the Corn Exchange. The Chichester Society kindly granted me permission to use an illustration from their 1986 Cattle Market Campaign booklet.

Finally many individuals have loaned me photographs of market-related activities, and I am very grateful to Anne Scicluna, Ken Green, Hugh Palmer and Geoffrey Claridge in this connection, and to Geoffrey Claridge goes special thanks for the excellent photograph he took for me of the revamped Market House.

To all these people I express my sincere gratitude, and I hope they enjoy reading the results of their kindness.

Illustration acknowledgements

Author's collection: 1, 5-10, 12-15, 18, 20, 23, 25-7, 32, 37, 39, 41, 49-51, 53-5, 58, 67-8, 75, 78-9, 81, 85, 87, 104-6, 109-10; 4, 28-30, 56, 76, 99, 102 (all courtesy Chichester District Museum); 60 (courtesy Pat Combes); 111 (courtesy Stride & Son)
Dean and Chapter, Chichester Cathedral: 48
Chichester District Museum: 2, 73, 77, 80, 83-4, 86, 107; 98 (courtesy *Chichester Observer*)
The Chichester Society: 97
Geoffrey Claridge: 35-6, 38
Pat Combes: 64-6
Mary Gostling: 108
Ken Green collection: 72
Simon Kitchen: 96
Ordnance Survey: 94
Hugh Palmer, courtesy Chichester District Museum: 95
David Sadler collection: 19, 61-3
Anne Scicluna: 90-2
Nick Stride: 88
Stride & Son, Chichester: 89, 93, 100-1
John Wiley and Sons: 44
WSRO: Frontis, 3, 11, 16-17, 21-2, 31, 33-4, 40, 42, 45-7, 52, 57, 69-71, 74, 82, 103; 43 and 59 (courtesy Geoffrey Claridge)

Introduction

MARKET-TOWN (mar´-kit-toun.) *s.* a town that has the privilege
of a stated market, not a village.

Stephen Jones, A General Pronouncing and Explanatory
Dictionary of the English Language, London, 1798

Chichester's development into the prosperous city it is today rests
on three important factors. Firstly it was a market town (and had
been since Roman times), secondly the moving of the see from Selsey
to Chichester in 1075 turned it into a cathedral city, and thirdly it was
once a thriving port. Chichester was anything but a village in 1798 when
Mr Jones penned his definition of 'market town'! The final accolade came
much later, in 1889, when it acquired the status of a county town on the
partitioning of Sussex into East and West.

The fertile Sussex coastal plain with the Downs behind ensured that
agriculture was the principal employer in the area, where farmers needed
the means to trade their produce and livestock; Chichester hosted several
markets to cater for this need. In addition local traders who did not own
their own shops needed a pitch to sell their wares, which resulted in the
famous Market Cross, erected at the intersection of the four main streets,
and a succession of three market houses in North Street.

For centuries all the markets were held in the streets, something that
was inconvenient for both traders and buyers alike (not to mention poor
passers-by on beast market days) and dissatisfaction with this led, in the
19th century, to the construction of purpose-built market facilities. The
first of these was a new Market House in North Street which was opened
by the corporation in 1808. The building popularly (but quite erroneously)
known as the Butter Market today was designed by the eminent architect
John Nash, but much altered in the early 20th century.

The second facility was the Corn Exchange, the Greek Revival temple that still dominates the East Street scene. Curiously this facility was not provided by the corporation (who seemed to have no time for the corn market) but was built as a private venture. Equally curious is the fact that this was the only one of Chichester's public buildings not to have been a subject for the late Francis Steer's Chichester Papers, possibly on account of the first and last minute books having gone missing. Fortunately I have managed to piece together its early story from other sources, and the chequered career of this venture is able to be told here – in some detail – for the first time.

A vigorous and acrimonious public campaign against the beast market being held in the streets eventually resulted in the last of the new facilities, the Cattle Market, which, when it opened in 1871 on open ground beyond Eastgate Square, meant that at last all vestiges of the markets had vanished from the streets, although cattle, sheep and pigs continued to be driven through the town to reach the new venue.

Sadly all these market facilities have ceased to trade; the Market House and Corn Exchange buildings have been put to other uses while the Cattle Market site has been turned into a car park. The Market Cross, redundant now for over 200 years, still stands at the centre of the city as an impressive, and iconic, reminder of Chichester's past as a market town.

Alongside the markets five ancient annual fairs were held in various locations about the city, of which only one – Sloe Fair – now survives, but in a form that is a far cry from its original calling, since trading at it no longer takes place.

In this book I have attempted to pull together the history of all these markets and fairs over the last 900 years and look at their effects, both social and economic, upon the city at large. Over the last five centuries many visitors and residents have written down their impressions of Chichester, and, perhaps not surprisingly, the markets and fairs frequently feature in these. I have sprinkled the text with quotations from these writings to add some contemporary spice to the documentary research.

Alan H.J. Green
Chichester, 2011

ONE

Prelude: Agriculture and Chichester

Fair waved the golden corn ...

A market town requires a constant source of – primarily – agricultural produce to trade, and so it is appropriate to commence this study of Chichester's markets with a look at the history of agriculture in this part of Sussex, in order to appreciate the background against which the various market facilities in Chichester developed.

Chichester was surrounded by fertile agricultural land ideal for the growing of grain crops and James Dallaway, in his monumental *History of Western Sussex* published in 1815,[1] comments upon the flourishing state of the corn trade at the end of the 17th century:

> The corn markets, when the trade of malting and exporting to Ireland was at its zenith, was more considerable than that of any provincial town in the south of England. Fuller (who wrote in 1660 and gives his authority) reveals that 'it is sufficient evidence of the plenty of this county that the tables of wheat, corne [*sic*] and malt growing or made about, or sold in the City of Chichester doth amount yearly at a halfpenny a quarter,* to sixty pounds and upwards (as the gathering thereof will attest) and the number of bushels† we leave to be audited by better arithmeticians. So I was informed by Mr Peckham, the Recorder at Chichester.

The work quoted by Dallaway was Fuller's *Worthies of England – Sussex*, published in 1662. In the 1660s the corn trade in Chichester, according to this contemporary source, amounted to some 28,000 quarters a year. The

---

* A quarter is the volumetric measure formerly used in corn trading which equates to 291.2 litres in metric units. This is not to be confused with the imperial unit of weight, also known as a quarter, which is a quarter of a hundredweight.

† A bushel is one eighth of a volumetric quarter; equivalent to eight gallons or 36.4 litres in metric units. It was standardised thus in 1824 by Act of Parliament, which eliminated the slightly smaller Winchester bushel that was in use in some places.

malt-growing to which he refers is the growing of barley for conversion into malt for use in brewing. Barley grown especially for malting had to have its protein content kept low by restrictive use of fertilisers; the thin soils of the chalk downs doubtless proved most useful in this respect.[2] Malting was once a not inconsiderable industry in Chichester, processing as it did the barley taken straight from the corn market. In 1662 there were no fewer than 10 malthouses within the city walls, whose combined output far exceeded the needs of the city's breweries, hence the need to export the surplus via Dell Quay.[3]

Another local Georgian historian, Alexander Hay, wrote a famous *History of Chichester*, published in 1804, and in it he made this contemporary observation about Chichester's agriculture at the dawn of the 19th century, referring to a 17th-century Act of Parliament that paid a bounty of 5s. per quarter on all wheat exported out of the kingdom:

> As Chichester is not, and never was to any great degree, a manufacturing town, or of extensive trade, it is evident it must depend for its prosperity on the country around it. It was sometime before this wholesome law operated even among the farmers, so as to produce any visible change for the better; and still longer ere these effects circulated to the market towns with which they were connected. Its first effect was that it secured to the cultivator of the land a certain market for his grain, and this security, in time, encouraged him to plough and sow with confidence – and in the issue enabled him, by the increase of his stock, to increase the produce of his lands. It is no extravagant conjecture to suppose that there is at this present time, thrice the quantity of grain produced in this neighbourhood as there was an hundred years ago … Many gentlemen and noblemen have of late commenced [being] extensive farmers, or rather agriculturalists, but it is not hitherto apparent that the practice has conduced, or is likely to conduce, to the good of the public, the production of an increased quantity of the necessities of life. If we allow as we ought, that they are more likely to make experiments than the regular farmer; on the other hand, it has been observed that their speculations have been directed to grazing and the rearing of cattle &c rather than the raising of grain, the public utility of their exertions may justly be doubted; as it is a fact that the produce of one acre of wheat will go as far in supporting the life of man as twelve acres laid out in rearing and feeding of cattle and sheep.[4]

When he wrote this Hay was reflecting both the advances made in agricultural science in the 18th century and the increase in farm sizes being brought about by the use of Enclosure Acts. One of the most important technical advances made was the Norfolk system of crop rotation, where successive crops of wheat, roots, barley or oats and grass with clover followed each other, increasing the productivity of the soil. By 1800 wheat was the predominant grain being grown in the south of England, the average yields of this crop increasing from 0.48 to 0.58 tons per acre between 1770 and 1836.[5]

The breeding of animals for slaughter and dairying had always been a feature of farming in the Chichester area, filling an essential link in the food chain, but what Hay was predicting about farmers moving more towards husbandry and cutting back on the growing of wheat became true as the 19th century wore on.

Trouble on the farm

The buoyancy of the corn trade was disturbed at the end of the 18th century by a series of bad harvests, leading to shortages of grain and an inevitable increase in the price of bread. In 1795 Prime Minister Pitt suggested in the Commons that MPs should set an example by reducing their consumption of bread, in order that more might be left for the use of the poor. He was lampooned for this, and that year there were riots around the country protesting at the price increases. The poor harvests hit farmers particularly hard: not only did they have little grain to sell, but they could not afford to buy the bread needed by their families.

The rioting even took place in sedate Chichester in 1795, as John Marsh, the city's great Georgian diarist, recorded:

> On the Friday follow'g the Hereford Militia who had been the ring-leaders in the late riot in Chichester, left it and march'd towards Newbury. Chichester was however by no means singular in shewing this riotous disposition, as at many other places the same was manifested particularly at Brighton where in the preceding week there had been a great tumult & a large quantity of grain destroyed (by way of making it <u>cheaper</u>) of which the principal ringleaders were the Oxford Militia, the privates of w'ch stood to their arms with fix'd bayonets against their officers & the magistrates, but were at length subdued by a piece or 2 of ordinance being fired just over their heads, which striking several of the bayonets disarm'd many of them & threw the rest into such confusion that they were soon vanquish'd & entirely disarm'd.[6]

From this we can see that the lower ranks of the various militias actually encouraged the rebellions rather than quelling them, as doubtless they too were hit by the shortage of the staff of life.

The end of the Napoleonic wars in 1815 brought about another period of depression and agricultural disturbance. The wars had taken away vast numbers of agricultural workers and many returned to find their jobs gone. Threshing machines had been introduced from 1800 to compensate for the lack of labour, and this operation, which previously had provided about three months of winter manual work, could now be completed by machine in a few weeks. Furthermore farmers were moving away from the old practice of employing live-in labourers to hiring men on a day-wage basis, so year-round employment was no longer guaranteed.[7]

More bad harvests plunged the country into further economic difficulties, with rapidly rising food prices, and the farm labourers, traditionally the lowest-paid of all workers, were thus doubly hit, and forced to rely on the inadequate help provided by the overloaded parish poor-rate system. The government tried to combat the problems by introducing a new Corn Law in 1815, which banned imports of cheap foreign grain until the home price had reached 80s. a quarter. This proved a two-edged sword: while it attempted to protect the home market, it deprived the poor of the cheap bread they so desperately needed – and yet more riots ensued.

Some labourers emigrated to Canada in the hope of escaping the poverty by starting a new life, and Lord Egremont of Petworth assisted (if that is the right word, for he really wished to reduce the burden on the poor rate) 1,456 souls to do so over a five-year period.[8]

Discontent with this enforced poverty was reflected in radicalism stirred up by agitators such as William Cobbett. Cobbett was born in 1762, the son of a Farnham innkeeper-cum-farmer, and developed radical ideas from observing the sufferings of the post-war depression. He carried out a tour of England – his *Rural Rides*, as he called them – addressing packed meetings and encouraging revolt among workers. He visited Sussex in 1822 and 1823, but the closest he got to Chichester was Singleton, where he stayed in August 1823.[9]

The weather continued to provide problems for farmers in southern England, where another series of poor harvests began in 1827 and a particularly severe winter of 1829-30 was followed by a cold and wet summer.

The misery and discontent culminated in the so-called Swing Riots, which broke out in the autumn of 1830 in Kent, quickly spreading into Sussex. The targets of the rioters were farmers, who were seen as being the villains of the piece in keeping wages low. Sussex saw 103 incidents (28 per cent of the national total), in which the commonest form of protest was arson against the hated threshing machines, together with hayricks and barns, often – perversely – destroying the fruits of the harvests and thus exacerbating the shortages. The rioters often also besieged the local parsons, seeking a reduction in the tithes they had to pay. The arsonists sent threatening letters to farmers always signed with the *nom de plume* Captain Swing so as to maintain anonymity. The identity of this Captain Swing – if he did actually exist – was never discovered, but William Cobbett was often suspected of being the ring-leader, although it could not be proved.

On Wednesday 17 November 1830 strangers who seemed to have no business to transact were observed among the farmers and traders attending the Chichester beast and corn markets. There were also reports of large groups of men gathering at Goodwood and Pagham, and the suspicions aroused were sufficient for magistrates to assemble a band of 50 men, hastily sworn in as special constables, who managed to disperse them quietly. However, that night 12 threshing machines were destroyed within a radius of a few miles of the city, and the next day eight men charged with arson were brought before Chichester magistrates sitting in the Council House. They were sent to the Petworth house of correction.[10]

More change

The Swing Riots in Sussex were largely over by the end of January 1831, but they spread to other parts of the country and the unrest lasted into 1832. After that conditions began to improve, and as the weather settled down and tempers cooled, yields of corn increased, rising to a peak in trade in 1871.[11] Unfortunately the 1870s witnessed another agricultural depression, one that ended the golden age of wheat-growing in Sussex for good. The complicated Corn Laws had been repealed in June 1846, leaving only a nominal duty on imported grain, but that was abolished completely in 1869. In the early 1870s imports of cheap wheat from Canada and the USA, now free of duty, began to pour into the country as advances in the size and speed of ships made such trade economically viable. Grain prices fell as a result.

In 1879 and 1880 there were disastrous harvests in Sussex, and farmers faced ruin as they were unable to compete with the ever-growing cheap imports. As a result they put much of their land over to grass and increased their stocks of sheep and cattle, meaning that Sussex ceased to be a major wheat-growing county.[12] H. Rider Haggard, best known by generations of O-level English candidates for *King Solomon's Mines*, was also keenly interested in agriculture and carried out a survey in 1901-2 of the state of the industry, published in two volumes. He visited several farms in Sussex, including that of Mr Pitts, who farmed 500 acres 'on the outskirts of Chichester'.* Mr Pitts was now predominantly a dairy farmer but also had a flock of Southdown sheep. Rider Haggard recorded that Mr Pitts 'did not seem enthusiastic or confident as to the position of the industry, since he remarked of the farmers in the district that they were all hard hit'.[13]

The change in the use of agricultural land is demonstrated by figures published in a report of 1911:[14]

Acreages of Sussex as arable and grasslands

Year	Arable	Grass
1872	388,849	262,578
1909	237,567	422,632

* This was Fred Pitts who, directories show, was at East Broyle Farm.

In other words there had been a 39 per cent drop in arable use of land in the county over 37 years.

The First World War brought logistical difficulties in securing imports, resulting in an edict from the government that more land should be made over to the growing of crops rather than being left to grass, as there was now a guaranteed market. This state of affairs was short lived, however, for after the war much agricultural land returned to grassland.[15] The growing of grain crops in Sussex continued to decline, as this extract from a description of Chichester in 1929 by R. Thurston Hopkins demonstrates:

> In Victorian days it was corn, cattle and clerics, but the corn has almost been eliminated. It does not pay to grow corn in Sussex today. Only a while ago a Sussex farmer told me that he could sell his corn straw at a better price than the grain it produced, and later I received a letter from a Canadian friend who wrote: 'We have settled down to work now in earnest and are breaking into a belt of wheat that runs back for twenty unbroken miles!' It is probable that the future will have no place with the past labours of the cornlands in Chichester, and the delicate bouquet of good Sussex wheat will be forgotten for ever.[16]

Thurston Hopkins gives the principal reason for the decline, namely the vast wheat fields of Canada; it would have been very difficult for Sussex farmers to envisage a single field of the size described, which would have stretched all the way from Chichester to Worthing. Not for nothing was Canada referred to as 'the breadbasket of the world'.

Husbandry

The declining arable farming in Sussex was replaced by husbandry, especially the rearing of sheep for both wool and meat. The principal breed was the Southdown, an ancient native breed that had become suited to life on the chalk downs. At the end of the 18th century John Ellman of Glynde refined the breed by internal selection rather than outcrossing, and exhibited his sheep at the Smithfield Show in 1799. The breed was exported to New Zealand, the place that in the 20th century was most associated with lamb for the table. High concentrations of sheep on the downs also helped with cropping, for they were folded in small areas to manure and tread the light chalky soil in preparation for planting the next year.[17]

The growth in sheep husbandry was rapid, and writing in 1813 the Rev. Arthur Young estimated that there were 200,000 ewes kept on the eastern South Downs. He said of Sussex farmers that 'the amazing number they keep is one of the most singular circumstances in the husbandry of England'.[18]

Walter Stride, who in the 1920s inherited his father's auctioneer's business in East Street, Chichester, and was thus heavily involved with

1 *A view of Westgate Fields in the 1940s, with bullocks grazing right up to the city walls. This land was also used to hold cattle before and after sale in the Cattle Market. The Avenue de Chartres has destroyed this image of* rus in urbe.

the Cattle Market, went on to become secretary of the Southdown Sheep Society. When he moved the business from East Street to 10 St John's Street in 1937 he renamed the building Southdown House in honour of his favoured breed. In 1950, 10 St John's Street was listed as being the office of the Southdown Sheep Society.[19]

The breeding of cattle increased after the First World War, largely with dairy herds in order to provide milk for the growing population. There was also the need for beef for the table and hides for tanning. To the south of Chichester, Westgate Fields, once the city's water meadows, had long been used for grazing of bullocks for beef, and up until 1964 Chichester could boast that cattle grazed right up to its city walls. Unfortunately the construction of the ring road (Avenue de Chartres) and the arrival of Chichester College, both in 1964, quickly brought about an end to this agrarian scene. Pigs also featured large in local husbandry, while the farmyard housed fowl in the form of chickens, turkeys, ducks and geese.

The Sussex County Show was held annually at different venues around the county, and the first to be held after the Second World War was staged in Chichester at Oaklands Park in July 1947. On the first day alone 13,643 people passed through the turnstiles to see the exhibits, which included 492 cattle entries – the second highest ever recorded – but only 44 sheep. The press steward for the Sussex County Agricultural Society pointed out that the fall-off in sheep entries was on account of the war, when many downland farmers had turned their land over to growing essential crops. Similarly the pig entries had been low.[20] The return to crop-growing seen in the First World War had resurfaced, but again only temporarily. Another wartime innovation was the growing of sugar beet in Sussex, and after the war this became well established north of Chichester – ensuring the survival of the railway between Chichester and Lavant, a stump of the former Chichester to Midhurst line that lost its passengers in 1935 and closed to freight beyond Lavant in 1953.

Horticulture

Those Cicestrians who had large gardens grew their own vegetables and probably kept a few hens to provide fresh eggs, but those blessed with less

2 *A Land Settlement Association smallholder at Keynor Farm, Sidlesham, with her prized pig, 1930s.*

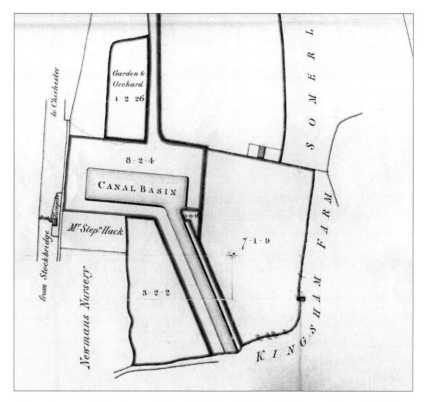

3 *A survey of lands owned by the Prebend of Bracklesham to the south of the city. Drawn up in 1821 to delineate land sold for the building of the canal, it shows Kingsham Farm, parcels of land occupied by Newman's Nursery and an orchard. At the time the canal basin was being built this part of the city was open countryside.*

space had to buy in such provisions from the markets. Supplies for these came from the many gardens, nurseries and orchards that surrounded the city. The land tax records for the lands outside the city walls give an insight into the large number of gardens and orchards that existed in the 18th and early 19th centuries. They also state that the site of the current cattle market had been an orchard.[21]

William Hoare, writing his memoirs in 1887, recalls that 'about 60 years ago' (*c.*1827) a nursery was broken up on the north-west side of the city to create what later became Orchard Street, his parents living in the first house that was built in Orchard Terrace at the Northgate end.[22] Orchard Street's only pub – alas long closed – was called the *Nursery Arms*.

Other sources of food were wild creatures, rabbits, hares and game, which were shot on the Downs and in the woods of local estates and brought to market.

4   *A Land Settlement Association produce basket from a Sidlesham smallholding, used to distribute mainly salad and fruit crops.*

In the 1930s the Land Settlement Association (LSA), a government-sponsored movement set up to give unemployed people – mainly ex-miners – a new start in horticulture, established 21 estates across England and Wales. In 1936 the LSA established such an estate at Sidlesham, south of Chichester. Some 800 acres of land were divided into smallholdings and the 'settlers' began arriving from the north in September.[23] They mostly produced salad and fruit crops, but pigs were also bred on the central farm at Keynor and most of the smallholders kept chickens.

The LSA was a co-operative, with sales and purchases organised centrally, so their goods did not get sold at the Market House; instead they were sent away by train in distinctive cardboard baskets. The LSA was wound up by the government in 1982 and the smallholdings were sold off to private growers.

TWO

Open all Weathers
The Markets in the Streets

> MAR'KET [*marche*, F, *mercatus*, L] a place where Provisions, or any Manner of Goods are set to Sale: The Privilege whereby a Town is enabled to keep a Market.
>
> N. Bailey, *An Universal Etymological English Dictionary*, London 1782

Chichester was a market town in Roman times, the forum having been at the bottom end of North Street on its west side. In the 12th century the markets belonged to the Earls of Cornwall, but the right to hold markets in the city was transferred to the citizens in 1316 and later enshrined in a charter granted to the city by King James II in 1685.[24] This lengthy document, which sets out how the city should be run, grants

> to the mayor, aldermen and citizens of the City of Chichester and their successors, that hereafter for ever, they may have and hold markets in every week, in the said City of Chichester, to wit, one on every Wednesday, and another on every Friday, and another on Saturday, to be held for ever.

The mayor of the day was appointed Clerk of the Market.[25] Another charter granted by James II two years later in 1687 made the same provisions.[26] When the Buck brothers produced their famous panoramic view of Chichester in 1738 they noted in the caption that 'The chief Traffick [*sic*] of the City is Corn and Cattle for both which the Markets here are as considerable as most in the Kingdom'. Praise indeed from artists who portrayed most of the principal cities in England and Wales in the early 18th century.[27]

However, despite the royal *imprimatur*, it was not until the 19th century that any adequate purpose-built market facilities were provided in Chichester. Before that all the markets catering for different commodities – animal and

5 *William Gardner's Chichester town plan of 1769. At the centre stands the Market Cross, given to the city in 1501 by Bishop Storey. At that time all the markets took place in the streets: the beast market was held in North and East Streets, the corn market and general market in North Street and the fish market in South Street. The markets frequently spilled over into West Street, much to the concern of the Dean and Chapter. Running north from East Street is St Martin's Lane, where once the hog market was held, and the church indicated 'D' was once known as St Martin in the Pig Market. Behind the buildings on the north side of East Street the church marked 'C' was known as St Andrew in the Oxmarket. Shambles Alley, home to the meat market, runs between North Street (by the 'N' in the street name) through to St Martin's Lane, emerging by St Martin's Church. The letter 'I' denotes the Council House of 1731 that housed the general and corn markets beneath it. Outside the city walls, to the north-west, are nurseries and orchards growing produce for the market.*

vegetable – were held in the streets as the medieval city had not developed a market-place to replace the Roman forum. In the case of the beast markets this was not to the general good of the shopping community, who had to cope with the resulting ordure and stampeding animals.

In the Georgian period market days were Wednesdays and Saturdays, the Friday market having ceased. The general market was held every Wednesday and Saturday and the beast market every other Wednesday.

The corn market was also held on Saturday, but by 1804 it had been moved to coincide with the beast market.[28] The markets were managed by the corporation, who provided some basic facilities for the fish and meat traders and charged tolls and dues to pay for them. In 1698 the tolls of the 'Marketts belonging to this City' were leased, probably experimentally, to Nathaniel Sowton for a period of three years, but by the 1790s it was the responsibility of the town crier and the gaoler to collect the market dues from traders.[29]

The Market Cross

Undoubtedly the most iconic of all Chichester's buildings is the medieval Market Cross. The history of this structure has been well documented, particularly so in an Otter Memorial Paper published in 2001 to mark its 500th anniversary.[30] As the Market Cross was rendered redundant by the opening of the new Market House in 1808, and thenceforward makes an exit from our market story,* only a résumé of its history is required here.

The cross was a gift made to the city in 1501 by Edward Storey, Bishop of Chichester from 1478 to 1503, in order to provide shelter for traders at the general market. Bishop Storey bought the land at the intersection of the four main streets, upon which it was to sit, from the corporation for £10 by an indenture dated 28 December 1501. The deed that established the cross stipulated that market traders using it would not be liable for any tolls or dues on their sales. Of hexagonal form, it is built of Caen stone, but, impressive as it is, it would not have sheltered very many traders.

6 *A charming naïve engraving of the medieval Market Cross, dated 1792 and by William Thomas after Nixon. The cross stands at the centre of the city and for 300 years housed the general market. In this view a butcher's shop can be seen on the corner of South and West Streets, while a shifty-looking character lurks in the shadows to the right.*

It does not appear to have been the first such structure on the site, for Alexander Hay, writing in 1804, states that Bishop Robert Read (alternatively spelled Rede) 'procured a cross of excellent workmanship to be set up in the market place' and records that the generous bishop departed this life in about 1417.[31] Earlier writers also refer to Read's cross; William Camden describing Chichester in about 1586 talks about a 'faire stone market place,

---

*   See Chapter Four.

7　An engraving of the Market Cross by J. Rogers after N. Whittock. It is dated 1829, by which time it had assumed its current form. The view is into West Street, where most of the buildings that once cut off the cathedral from the street still stand. The new Market House, which opened in 1808, had taken the traders away from the Market Cross, and iron railings have been inserted to close off the openings.

supported with pillars round about' as having been provided by him, but one has to wonder whether, as the description so closely matches Storey's cross, Read's name has become mistakenly associated with it.[32] This earlier cross, if it did exist, must have been demolished long before the present one was planned, otherwise the land would not have had to be purchased from the corporation by Bishop Storey.

8　As a symbol of trade, the Market Cross appeared on some Georgian trade tokens. This is a 1794 halfpenny payable at Dally's the tailors.

9　A souvenir bone china pin tray commissioned by Chichester City Council to mark the 500th anniversary of the Cross in December 2001.

10 *The re-enactment of the dedication ceremony on the 500th anniversary of the Market Cross on 28 December 2001 by the current Bishop of Chichester, the Very Rev. John Hind.*

Following its redundancy as a market facility in 1808, the Market Cross acquired a new role as – quite literally – the centre of the city, and the corporation then referred to it as the High Cross. Proclamations are made in front of it, revellers dance around it at New Year, preachers evangelise by it and the young use it as a convenient rendezvous. It has long been a hazard to traffic, but has survived many attempts at uprooting and replanting in some less disruptive location. Fortunately it is now Grade I listed and a scheduled ancient monument, so mercifully all fear of such Philistine threats should have receded.

In December 2001 the 500th anniversary of the Market Cross was marked with a re-enactment of the dedication ceremony, and a blue plaque – the first in Chichester – was placed on a building nearby to commemorate the event.

The Old Market Houses in North Street

The low capacity of the Market Cross was supplemented, at some undetermined date, by a market house built in North Street. This market house was a timber building that sat in the carriageway between Shambles Alley and Lion Street, and James Spershott* in his memoirs refers to it as the 'old corn market house'. No engraving of it exists, but Spershott provides us with a good description:

> [It] stood in the North Street on the west side; it was pretty long from south to north, one side of it was close to the gutter in the middle of the street and the other within about six or seven feet of the houses. It stood upon posts or fram'd timbers, panelled up about breast high. It had an entrance on each side, but its chief entrance was at the south end about half its width next the houses, the other half being the cage which was boarded up breast high and wood bars perpendicular above. Behind the cage was the stairs up into the council chamber which was low and had low old windows. It was a very old building. The north end was nearly opposite the south end of the new market house.[33]

---

*   James Spershott was born in Oving in 1710 of Baptist stock. He became a joiner by trade and a joint pastor of the Baptist chapel in Eastgate Square. He wrote his memoirs late in life (he died in 1789) and, even allowing for the fact that by then his memory may have been playing some tricks, they give a fascinating insight into Georgian Chichester.

At this time the functions of the city's town hall were split between this building and the Guildhall in what is now Priory Park. From Spershott's description the old market house can be inferred to have been similar to a building hailing from Titchfield in Hampshire that has been re-erected at the Weald and Downland Museum at Singleton. This too has a council house on the first floor above a semi-open trading area beneath. The Chichester building seems to have been used as a general market house when not required for the weekly corn market.

The City Fathers were obviously not enamoured with their town hall and the inconvenience of operating on a split site, for in 1728 they resolved that 'the Market House and Council House may be taken down and rebuilt in place and sufficient sum of money shall be raised by Gn subscription for the purpose'.[34] The council minutes of this era are frustratingly brief and do not record any discussion about the lot of the market traders who were to be transferred to the new premises.

The new building opened in 1731 to a design by Roger Morris – earlier designs by Lord Burlington, the Duke of Richmond's preferred architect, having been rejected.[35] It was built on the east side of North Street on the corner of Custom House Lane (now Lion Street) and, echoing the old building it replaced, the ground floor was left open to house market traders. Above it a most elegant council chamber was provided, which was far more fitting for a progressive Georgian city.

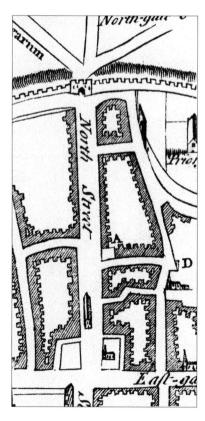

The old market house was pulled down in 1731 and no trace remains. Inside the council chamber of the new building is a board commemorating its completion. The citation begins: 'This Council House and Corn Market of the antient [sic] City of Chichester', implying that corn marketing, at least, was expected to continue beneath it.

11 *An extract from William Stuckeley's town plan of 1723, showing the old market and Council House that stood in the middle of the road in North Street. Its date of construction is not recorded, but it is shown on John Norden's town plan of 1595.*

12 *The restored early 17th-century market house at the Weald and Downland Museum, Singleton. It came from Titchfield in Hampshire, but gives an impression of what the one at Chichester might have looked like.*

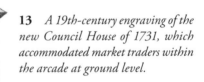

13 *A 19th-century engraving of the new Council House of 1731, which accommodated market traders within the arcade at ground level.*

14 *The space beneath the new Council House that was once used to house the corn and general markets. Today it serves as a sheltered entrance to the Assembly Rooms – which is most welcome on wet days.*

However, the Market Cross and the space beneath the new Council House between them still did not offer much space for markets, and so those who could not avail themselves of their shelter had to set up stalls in the streets and pray for fine weather. It would be another 77 years before adequate facilities were provided for the general market.

The fish and meat markets

The goods sold at the Chichester general markets included, naturally, much fresh fish. Samuel and Nathaniel Buck, in their aforementioned panoramic view of Chichester, also mention in the caption that the market 'was well supply'd with provisions of all sorts, particularly Shell Fish, Lobsters, Prawns and Crabbs being in utmost perfection here in proper season'. Strangely they did not mention the oysters that came from Emsworth, which at the time were considered among the best to be had in England.*

15 *Billingsgate Fish Market in London, c.1790. A fish wife sells her wares from a simple table with no canopy for weather protection, while others sell from baskets on their heads.*

The fish market was situated at the top end of South Street near the water conduit and was referred to as the fish shambles. Spershott recalls it in his memoir for 1777 as 'The fish shambles being made of stone before which were of wood'.[36] Mr Bailey, in his dictionary of 1782, defines 'shambles' as 'a Table, Board or Stall … where Flesh is laid for sale. A place where Butchers sit and sell meat.' We have no descriptions of what the Chichester shambles were like but they are quite likely to have resembled those seen in London, as illustrated in Fig. 15.

The fish shambles, too, was managed by the corporation, and in 1724 they were obviously experiencing some sort of revolt by Bosham fishermen who were bringing their wares to the market. On 2 June that year it was

> Ordered that the inhabitants of Bosham bringing ffish to the Marketts of this City shall [illegible] selfwith and sell the same at the lower end of the Shambles and must pay the Markett Toll or other dues as others selling fish in the said Markett and that the Common Cryer do give notice of this Order.[37]

---

* The Emsworth oyster industry famously came to an ignominious end in 1902, when bivalves bought there were ascertained to have been the cause of the death of the Dean of Winchester.

The fish shambles came to the forefront of their deliberations again in 1792, the year Chichester was finally properly paved. In June the fish market had to be moved temporarily southwards to facilitate the paving works and in July, when it returned, it was resolved that the fish shambles should be removed to the east side of the street. The shambles themselves were obviously renewed in August, for the decision was taken that they would be made of wood – the earlier stone ones presumably having been broken up – and this would have made them portable, which the earlier ones clearly were not. The following month the duty of putting out and taking down the shambles was put upon the town crier, for which he was to be paid an extra four guineas a year. Interestingly he had to put the shambles out at 6 a.m.[38]

There had also been a butchers' shambles in North Street, from which the name Shambles Alley doubtless derives, but it had closed by the middle of the 18th century. The building remained in the corporation's ownership and on 20 February 1756 it was leased to Judith Collins, being described as 'the messuage or tenement in the North Street, parcel of the tenement late called the Butchers' Shambles'.[39] The business had transferred to the new Council House, where in April 1785 it was ordered that 'stauls [sic] or shambles be erected in the room under the New Assembly Room for the Accommodation of out coming Butchers and that such Room be paved'.[40] The 'New Assembly Room' had been added to the rear of the council chamber in 1783, to a design by James Wyatt, replacing the old assembly rooms in North Pallant.[41]

The corn market

Farmers producing crops of barley, wheat or oats, then collectively known as corn, disposed of their produce to dealers, millers and maltsters at the weekly corn market. We have seen from the caption to the Buck brothers' *South-West Prospect of the City of Chichester* that the Chichester corn market was reckoned 'as considerable as most in the kingdom'.

Corn markets were quite different from the other markets and came in two forms – the sample market and the pitched market. In the former a farmer brought along a sample of his grain in a marked sack to tempt buyers into placing an order that would be delivered from the farmer's own granary. At a pitched market as much of the farmer's stock of grain as could be got onto a cart was brought along, with one sack being 'pitched' in the market-place for inspection; buyers could buy and take away as much or as little as they wished. For the buyers this method had the advantage that they could inspect the entire load to check the quality was consistent, but the poor farmer had to convey his stock to the market and then take home any that remained unsold at the end of the day – only to return with it the following week. As with the other markets, Chichester's corn market was held in the street, anciently in North Street, and, as we have seen, James Spershott refers to the medieval market house there as being the 'old corn market house'.[42]

After the old market house perished in 1731 the corn market continued to be held in North Street, as Alexander Hay records:

> Formerly the corn market was kept on Saturdays in the North Street: and sold in kind, not by sample. But lately, by the change of various circumstances, that way became inconvenient and almost impracticable. And therefore all the wheat, and nearly the whole of the business (of grain) is done by sample, and that principally on the beast market day instead of Saturday.[43]

From this we learn that by 1800 Chichester's means of corn trading had changed to a sample market; the inconvenience of the former pitched market, to which Hay alludes, was undoubtedly caused by there being no adequate covered space for the farmers' grain stocks. Although, as we have seen, the space beneath the new council house had been termed by the corporation 'the corn market', it was very restricted in size and would have been incapable of housing the corn market in its pitched form. In the early 1830s market trading reports carried by the *Hampshire Telegraph* refer to the Chichester corn market as being held at Northgate rather than North Street.

Despite its obvious importance, the corn market seems to have been something of a Cinderella in the corporation's eyes, for it hardly ever appears in the minutes of their deliberations, leaving us unsure as to how it was actually managed. The first extant council minute book was begun in 1685, and in the front are recorded all the oaths sworn by the various officials. One of these was the 'Corne Measurer', who undertook to undertake his office of measuring 'the quantities of Mault [*sic*], Wheat, Barley or other grain … faithfully, duly diligently and carefully'.

After that there is no further mention of the corn market until 1830. There was obviously a strong need for proper corn market facilities, but the corporation seemed oblivious to it. It had to be left to private enterprise to come up with the solution in the form of the Corn Exchange – as we shall see in Chapter Five.

THREE

'A Great Nuisance'
The Beast Market in the Streets

Joseph Gilbert's celebrated painting of East Street given in Fig. 16 captures a Chichester scene the passing of which few would surely lament – the beast market. By this time it was a mixed animal market, and the economic importance of it is captured by Alexander Hay writing in 1804:

> The beast market, holden every second Wednesday throughout the year invariably, for black cattle, sheep and hogs, is much the greatest of any in this or neighbouring counties, that of London excepted, not only the city, but the country for many miles around is supplied from thence. To it the Portsmouth butchers regularly resort – and not seldom the carcase butchers from London attend it. It is kept in East Street, the whole of which is occupied on markets days and more than half the North Street.[44]

There was also a horse market in North Street, established in 1709 by the corporation, which took place in the afternoon of every beast market day, with each seller paying a toll of 4d. for each horse sold.[45] Another contemporary account, which gives us a better idea of the geographical extent of the market, is provided by William Hoare (whom we met in Chapter One) in his memoirs of the early 19th century:

> the old cattle market when it was held in the streets … was a very large one. It used to occupy the East Street, North Street and a part of the West Street and I have seen a few in South Street. At that time there used to be from Little London to the East Walls posts and chains to tye [sic] the cattle too [sic].[46]

From this we see that the beast market was capable of spreading to the whole of the city centre on occasions.

16 *East Street, Chichester, 1814, an engraving after a painting by Joseph Gilbert, looking from the junction with North Pallant down to the Market Cross. This shows the fortnightly beast market, with sheep in pens being examined by farmers and another farmer trying to drive a small flock of sheep, three of whom are about to make a break for liberty into North Pallant. Some cattle are standing, apparently untethered, in the middle of the road, while two boys taunt the rather corpulent gentleman who provides the foreground focus of the picture.*

The 'great nuisance'

The view given in Gilbert's 1814 painting is seemingly more ordered than that which must have prevailed up to the late 1770s, for in December 1777 the mayor suggested at a meeting of the corporation that 'the penning of Hogs in the Beast Market of the City would remove a great nuisance'. This was agreed to, and it was ordered that four score wattles (i.e. hurdles) be provided for that purpose. The idea obviously worked, for many more wattles were ordered over subsequent years to accommodate sheep, and places were then needed to store the wattles between market days. Two stores were created in 1783, one under the East Walls to house the wattles used in East Street and one to the south of the Council House for those in North Street.[47]

On the subject of hogs, in earlier times the hog market had been held in what is now St Martin's Street. The street's previous appellation was Hog Lane, under which name it goes in early deeds, but by 1769, when Gardner's town plan was produced, it had become St Martin's Lane. The tiny church of St Martin* carried in the 13th century the rather unflattering dedication St Martin in the Pig Market. Adjoining the church was a pound provided by the corporation for the incarceration of those hogs who dared to escape captivity, but this was leased in 1767 to one James Beeding for the building of the detached house now numbered 21 St Martin's Square.[48] The precise date when the hog market was amalgamated with the sheep and cattle markets is unknown, but it had obviously happened before 1777 when the first of those wattles were purchased.

Another church with an agronomic dedication was St Andrew Oxmarket, situated behind the buildings on the north side of East Street and only accessible from it via two narrow twittens between the buildings. Its name suggests that the ox market once surrounded it, but I have found no evidence of this. Alison McCann, in her history of St Andrew's, is of the opinion that the name simply derived from its proximity to the East Street beast market.[49]

The task of putting the wattles out on market days, gathering them in again and carrying out running repairs fell to the gaoler and the town crier. In October 1798 it was agreed to pay them a joint bonus of £10 for providing this service, but 10 years later the town crier cried off the extra work. It was contracted instead to George Gatehouse, who undertook the service for the all-in fee of £60 a year.[50] For a short time from May 1792, while East Street was being paved, the beast market was held entirely in North Street, but this was obviously not deemed a success, for in September 1792 the City Fathers voted to keep the beast market permanently in East Street. The proviso to this was that the Paving Commissioners would erect posts and

AN

A C T

To regulate and improve the Cattle Market, to provide a Market House, and establish a Market for Sale of Butchers Meat and other Articles, and to make other Improvements, within the City of *Chichester*, in the County of *Sussex*.

[*Received the* ROYAL ASSENT, *8th August* 1807.]

WHEREAS the City of *Chichester*, in the County of *Sussex*, is an ancient and populous City, and a Market for the Sale of Live Cattle and Swine hath for divers Years last past been held in the said City on a certain Day in every other Week, in the East and North Streets of the same City, and the Body Corporate of the Mayor, Aldermen, and Citizens of the said City have, at their own Expence, provided and maintained all manner of necessary and proper Pens, Coops, and other Erections within the said Market, and certain Tolls have for divers Years last past been paid, and are now payable to the said Mayor, Aldermen, and Citizens, for the sale of Live Cattle and Swine within the said Market, nevertheless by reason of the want of sufficient and expeditious Means of Redress and Punishment, divers ill-disposed Persons, out of Wantonness and Malice, do frequently destroy the said Pens, Coops, and other Erections belonging to the said Market, to the great Injury of the said Market, and to the manifest Damage of the said Mayor, Aldermen, and Citizens, and Cattle are frequently negligntly and improvidently driven in the public Streets of the said City, and by reason thereof, not only the Persons frequenting the said Market, and buying and selling Cattle there, but also the Inhabitants of the said City, and others resorting thereto, are frequently exposed to great Danger:

126.   A   And

17 *The title page of the 1807 Chichester Markets Act, which provided powers for improving the regulation of the beast market and building a new market house.*

---

*   St Martin's Church was demolished in 1906; a charming walled garden now occupies the site.

rails to contain the market, the corporation being responsible for providing and removing them on market days.[51]

The inconvenience of markets being held in the streets was not entirely lost on the corporation, even though they always seemed loath to do anything about it. At a meeting of the Common Council on 17 December 1802 it was agreed that the holding of the market in different places was an 'inconvenience', and that it 'would be desirable to have the market in some fixed place'.[52] This laudable sentiment eventually led to the passing of an Act of Parliament in 1807, entitled 'An Act to regulate and improve the Cattle Market, to provide a Market House, and establish a Market for Sale of Butchers' Meat and other Articles, and to make other Improvements, within the City of Chichester, in the County of Sussex'.[53]

The main business of the Act was the building and running of a new market house, which we will look at in Chapter Four, but it also set out many new parameters for the regulation of what was now termed the 'cattle market' and solving some of the problems that beset it. In the preamble to the Act it was pointed out that the mayor and corporation had provided at their own expense 'all manner of necessary and proper Pens, Coops and other Erections' within the market, and levied tolls thereon. It then goes on to lament the fact that:

> nevertheless by reason of the want of sufficient and expeditious Means of Redress and Punishment, divers ill-disposed Persons out of Wantonness and Malice, do frequently destroy the said Pens, Coops and other Erections belonging to the said Market, to the great Injury of the said Market, and to the manifest Damage of the said Mayor, Aldermen, and Citizens, and Cattle are frequently negligently and improvidently driven in the public Streets of the said City, and by reason thereof, not only the Persons frequenting the said Market, and buying and selling Cattle there, but also the Inhabitants of the said City, and others resorting thereto, are frequently exposed to great Danger.

Lofty words indeed (and made even more poignant by the use of capital letters where one would not expect them), which reflect badly on the behaviour of visiting marketers and, presumably, some wayward citizens as well. Curiously, although the Act refers to cattle and swine, it makes no mention of the other kinds of animals sold in Chichester's market – sheep and horses.

The powers granted by the Act relating to the cattle market permitted levying a fine not exceeding £5 against those who failed to pay their tolls, and the bringing of those causing damage to the corporation's property before the Justice of the Peace to be prosecuted. The mayor and corporation were permitted to establish rules for the regulation of the markets and to alter them from time to time if needed. These remedial powers applied to the yet-to-be-built new Market House as well as the beast market, as we shall see in Chapter Four.

Another interesting provision in the Act allowed the corporation, instead of collecting the market tolls using its own employees, to let the tolls to a third party by auction or contract, for a period not exceeding three years. Under this, tenders could be sought from individuals who, in return for a fixed annual payment to the corporation, would extract the tolls and dues from the traders, pocket the same and hope to make a profit into the bargain. The downside of this early example of privatisation was that the successful bidder would also be responsible for absorbing any losses occasioned by traders who refused to pay up. In February 1824 it was decided to use this power and let the tolls of the beast market by auction, and the first 'renter of tolls' (as he was to be known) was Jack Holder, who bid £81 a year for the privilege and also paid for a new stock of wattles.*

The nuisance spreads

To the south of East Street a new residential development was begun in 1809 on the site of the former Blackfriars Friary, which at that time was the garden of a mansion house on the corner of Baffins Lane and East Street. The site had been divided into 60 building plots and sold by auction in 1808 by its owner, Major-General John Gustavus Crosbie of Funtington. The development was known as the New Town† and comprised the three streets now known as St John's Street, New Town and Friary Lane. Crosbie put restrictive covenants into the sales indentures in an attempt to secure a measure of exclusivity attractive to the better sorts of resident. The site was extra-parochial on account of its having been a friary, and so the corporation did not have responsibility for paving or scavenging the streets, the costs of providing these services falling to the non rate-paying proprietors.[54]

Inevitably, inquisitive cattle strayed from the beast market to explore this new territory, giving rise to complaints to the corporation, who resolved on 13 December 1822

---

* Strangely, although this resolution was passed on 1 February 1824, there is no mention in the Common Council minute books of the subsequent award of the contract. It was not until 24 February 1837, when a sub-committee was charged to investigate the history of the letting of market tolls, that we learn the name of Mr Holder and the amount of his tender. Perversely the sub-committee reported that the cattle market tolls were first let in 1823 – the year before the resolution to do so was passed! (Ref WSRO C/5 Common Council minute book 1827-35.)

† In the early days the development was known as the New Town but confusion was caused when the middle street, originally Cross Street, was renamed New Town, so the area became known as Newtown. We then had a street called New Town in an area known as Newtown!

18 *An extract from Fuller's town plan of 1820 showing the New Town development on the site of the former Blackfriars Friary, which began building in 1809. The streets marked George Street, Cross Street and St John's Street were intended to be an exclusive development for the professional classes. The proximity to the beast market in East Street to the north was a source of nuisance to its new residents.*

19 *A Victorian view of the beast market in East Street looking east, with the 1832 Corn Exchange dominating the view. Although not in good condition, this early photograph (probably late 1860s) shows the chaos that ensued, with sheep in pens and cattle wandering about in the road in front of the Corn Exchange, beyond which the entrance to St John's Street can be seen.*

that posts and chains be fixed on both sides of St John's Street in the New Town to prevent beasts getting on the pavement, and that a committee consisting of the mayor, John Newland, John Murray, Ric. Murray, Wm Humphry and James Powell or any three of them should give directions for the same to be done in a way satisfactory to the proprietors of property in the New Town.[55]

The work was obviously not carried out, for there is no further mention of it in the Common Council minute book. Indeed, since the streets of the New Town were not the corporation's responsibility anyway, one has to wonder why on earth they proposed putting posts and chains down the lengths of both sides of St John's Street to keep the beasts off the pavements. Surely it would have been more sensible just to chain off the end of the street, to stop cattle entering in the first place! It should also be noted that Richard Murray was a proprietor of the New Town development, and so this proposal should have given rise to a conflict of interest.

It was left to the Newtown proprietors to take the matter into their own hands, which they did in 1825. On 4 October that year they drew up an agreement:

> We the undersigned Proprietors of St John's Street and other parts of the extra-parochial lands within the walls of the City of Chichester called New Town at a meeting held this day at the house of Mr James Rogers do order that posts and chains be erected at the West and North ends of the street in the same New Town to prevent the cattle on market days from entering and filling up the same – and Mr Wingham and Mr Atkey having consented to direct the necessary operations they are to appoint two persons to attend the said chains so that passengers requiring to enter the streets may not be interrupted and that the expense of the above shall be paid by a rate.[56]

The Newtown proprietors had solved the problem by the more pragmatic means of chaining off the ends of St John's Street and Cross Street, thus keeping the cattle out altogether and – rightly – at their own expense.

Discontent begins to emerge

From 1835 the beast market tolls were let to Mr Ginman, who managed to remain the renter of tolls, mostly by negotiation rather than tender, for a series of three-year terms until 1840. The management of the beast market obviously continued to be chaotic, for at the meeting of the Common Council on 9 November 1836 Alderman Benness Adames* proposed a motion to appoint a committee to 'examine and ascertain what arrangements can be made for the better accommodation of Cattle and Sheep on the Cattle Market Days'. As always, the results of such investigations took a long

---

* Benness Adames was a hatter, linen and woollen draper, whose shop was in East Street.

time to come to fruition, and it was not until February 1837 that, under the 1807 Act, it was agreed with Mr Ginman to 'regulate' the market. Fat stock would be penned in East Street, lean stock in the upper part of North Street, calves opposite the Council Chamber and swine in the lower part of North Street.[57] There is no mention of where the sheep were to be billeted.

Mr Ginman's reign came to an end in March 1840 when he was outbid to the tune of £7 by Thomas Lipscombe, who tendered £110 a year and was appointed 'Contractor for the Cattle Market'. New regulation measures were forced upon him immediately, this time regarding the times at which the wattles were put up, and the penning of sheep. The additional regulations obviously failed to satisfy those trading at the beast market, for a 'memorial' (i.e. a petition) signed by 23 farmers and others was read out to the Common Council meeting on 9 November 1841:

> To the Town Council of the City of Chichester.
>
> We the undersigned Farmers and Graziers frequenting of the City of Chichester Stock Market beg to represent to your notice the great inconvenience to which we are subjected in consequence of want of room and proper accommodation for Stock particularly with regard to the Cattle Market. And we request you will take the subject into your early consideration with a view to remedy the Evils complained of – we are ready and willing to cooperate with you in any manner which will appear calculated to effect the objects you may have in view.[58]

In response a Cattle Market Committee was elected, consisting of the mayor and four other aldermen, to investigate the allegations. Taking their time as ever, they reported back to the meeting on 7 June 1842. Their opinion was that 'it is not at present advisable to alter or interfere with the present mode of conducting the market'. The response of the petitioners is not recorded, but the following year the rules of the market were amended again, which included regulating the hour at which selling could commence, namely 3 a.m. between 31 March and 1 October and 5 a.m. for the following half-year, with no animals being brought into the city before these times. Although long trading hours might have been good for business they were far from ideal for those living in North and East Streets or on the main trade routes thereto, whose slumbers would have been disturbed every market day.[59]

All through this period the Common Council minute books record regular expenditure on repairs to the cattle market posts and chains, suggesting they took more than their fair share of rough treatment. The frequency of the market had remained fortnightly, but in February 1846 a new Cattle Market Committee was set up, charged with entering into communication with any committee that users of the market might appoint to investigate a need for a weekly market instead. Nothing more is recorded of the proposal, so it was obviously dropped.[60]

The burgeoning size of the East Street market was such that by 1857 it was necessary to extend it into Eastgate Square, for which more moveable posts and chains were provided to keep the animals off the pavements. In addition the corporation experimented with allowing cattle to stand in the road along East Walls as far as the archway through the Roman wall. The following year 12 citizens complained about the late hours being kept by the horse dealers, but this at least was dealt with by means of a bylaw.[61] The misery caused to the general public by the beast market was being allowed to spread willy-nilly, and as a result resentment was mounting.

The citizens strike back

It is manifest that in all their deliberations about the running of the beast market, the mayor and corporation gave little, if any, consideration to the inconvenience it caused to the general public. Indeed they had obviously chosen to ignore one particular protest brought to their attention in a revealing 'memorial' that was read out at the council meeting on 7 July 1859:

> Chichester June 30th 1859
>
> Mr Mayor & Gentlemen
>
> Some time ago a Protest signed by the Bishop, the Dean, the Canon in Residence, Dr McCarogher, Dr Tyacke, Mr W.H. Freeland, Mr C.J. Jones, Revd G. Braithwaite and Revd T. Brown against the introduction of the Beast Market into the West Street was intrusted [*sic*] to Mr E.W. Johnson for presentation to the Municipal Authorities of our city having jurisdiction in such matters. What became of that Protest or how it was received, we have never learned. We regret to have to complain that the nuisance against which we have protested has not been abated, but rather increased since that time. On several recent occasions sheep have been kept for some hours within three yards of the West gates of the Cathedral Yard. We therefore deem it right to invite your attention to this encroachment and respectfully beg that you will exercise your authority for the future prevention of that breach of the law of which we complain.
>
> We have the honour to be,
>
> > Mr Mayor and Gentlemen
> > Your Obedient Servants.[62]

It was signed by eight prominent citizens, including the bishop and a certain Canon C.A. Swainson, of whom more anon.

Despite the nine gentleman listed in the petition's opening sentence being prominent members of the clerical, medical and legal professions, their protest had not officially reached the council, for there is no record of it in the minutes, suggesting that perhaps the mayor had dismissed it as unworthy of consideration. The mayor at this time was Charles

20 *A view of the Market Cross looking west, with a flock of sheep being driven towards the market. In 1840, when this view was made, all animals were driven to market on the hoof, thereby spreading the inconvenience across the whole city.*

Townsend Halsted, who ran the successful iron foundry Halsted & Sons, between North and East Pallants. His management style there was somewhat tyrannical, and it would seem that he carried this across to his running of the council.[63] The town clerk was instructed to write to the Revd G. Braithwaite acknowledging receipt of the memorial which had been 'laid before the council', but that is as far as it went: once again no action was taken. Five years later this inaction caused the Rev. Thomas Brown to petition the Privy Council on the matter of the West Street market, and a sternly worded letter was sent to the council by the Privy Council's medical officer, which was read to the meeting of 5 July 1864. At last they were being forced to sit up and take notice.

The next protest came from a private citizen, William Dilke, who on 15 July 1864 wrote a lengthy letter to the mayor complaining that the beast market in North Street was blocking the carriage approach to his house 'with a double row of cattle pens from one o'clock pm on Tuesday, at which time they were put in position, until 5pm on Wednesday'. He goes on to allude to an earlier complaint he had made, which had been ignored, and pointed out that when he bought his house the market was never held in front of it and that if nothing was done to remove the grievous nuisance he would be forced to 'take all lawful and proper means to rid myself of it'. Dilke lived at what is now 61 Greyfriars, and his complaint reveals that the beast market was extending further up North Street as well as into West Street: the whole town centre was becoming engulfed by it.

As a result of Dilke's letter another market committee, consisting of the mayor and two aldermen, was set up to investigate the problem. The result of their deliberations was an approach to the Corn Exchange Company asking whether the two 'avenues' alongside the Corn Exchange might be used for housing fatstock on market days, to which proposal the company willingly agreed for a mere £20 a year, provided no pigs or sheep were brought onto their premises. Strangely the company agreed to provide the posts and rails and to clean up afterwards – but then they never did show much business acumen, as we shall see in Chapter Six.[64] The council wrote to the medical officer at the Privy Council explaining that the arrangement with the Corn Exchange Company would solve the problems (and also refuting allegations that wells were being polluted as a result of the street market), but unfortunately the arrangement was never implemented. The following May the council withdrew from the arrangement, as the Corn Exchange Company had not provided the posts and rails in accordance with the agreement.[65]

Next to join the protest were members of Chichester's medical profession. They had approached the General Board of Health with a one and a half page letter listing the hazards to the health of citizens posed by the beast market, and campaigning to have it removed from the streets. It was signed by 13 doctors, including Dr Tyacke, who had been active in the 1859 West Street campaign. They also sent an even longer memorial to the mayor and corporation, which was read out at the council meeting of 4 April 1865. The transcript, which takes up three pages in the minute book, begins:

> After the unanimous Declaration of the whole of the enlightened Medical Staff of the City that the impurities of the Cattle Market held within the City are 'highly injurious' to the health of the inhabitants, we owe it to ourselves and families most earnestly to appeal to you for relief from this increasing and oppressive Evil as speedily as may be by removing the Cattle Market to a more suitable district.

On it goes in similar vein, to complain of overcrowding, the profane language of the drovers,* injuries to animals and escaping beasts posing dangers to the public. It cites an editorial in the *Daily Telegraph*, which expressed astonishment 'that Chichester should retain a custom that is so singularly behind the country'. It also tells the case of poor Mr Parvin, who was gored to death in the street, and how on the previous market day some 'wild animals' had rushed into a shop and got so firmly wedged behind the counter that the said counter had to be dismantled in order

---

* An occupational hazard in that line of business.

to free them. The memorial carried a copy of the petition to the General Board of Health and was signed by no fewer than 62 citizens, including Dr Tyacke and our Mr Dilke of North Street.

The following year, 1866, was not a good one for the mayor and corporation. A national outbreak of what was termed 'cattle plague' (actually the deadly rinderpest respiratory and gut disease) caused the beast market to be closed from 16 April to 1 June for the sale of cattle, and then Canon Swainson added his opinions to what was fast becoming a national disgrace with the publication of a fiery 25-page pamphlet entitled 'A Few Words to those who have the welfare of Chichester at Heart'. Opening with the rhetorical question 'Who are the people that want to ruin Chichester?', he goes on to condemn the City Fathers, alleging that 'The policy of our Rulers and the majority of our Town Council is to crush all expression of discontent. But we will not be crushed; we will make ourselves heard.' There were two thrusts in his campaign: the provision of a sewerage system and the removal of the cattle market from the streets. We will concern ourselves only with the latter, where Swainson accuses the mayor and corporation of ignoring public opinion (which, as we have seen, they clearly had) and, *inter alia*, flagrant breaches of the law and illegal trespass when they extended the market into West Street onto land they did not own. He also delivers the most damning description of the beast market so far:

> The streets are quiet enough for eleven working days in the fortnight, but on the twelfth it says that the man of business shall not know how long he shall want to catch his train; it compels everyone to drive by the Cross, and the two streets that lead to the Cross are absolutely impassable ... Even to drive into the chief stables in East Street from the country, you subject your horses to the danger of being gored by some cattle in their market day perplexities. Thus for one day in twelve (I put aside Sundays) the Chichester shops are inaccessible. Indeed one cannot drive up to the shop doors on the previous afternoon because of the pens. And it is no better on Wednesday afternoon – no one can have forgotten how the Duke of Richmond's waggonette was upset in East Street in 1861, and the ladies thrown out. And if beast-market day is a wet day, as it very often is, the next two days are almost as bad. The cattle and sheep and pigs stand in their own filth for so many hours that, when at last they are moved and driven off, they leave their marks behind on the pavement and there they may often be seen until the Sunday morning; for it is of the essence of our local non-governors neither to clean the pavements themselves, nor to require the householders to do so. Indeed the latter would be unjust. And thus it is a fact that the better-dressed people avoid Chichester, not only on the market-day but on two or three days after. Thus, so far as they are concerned, the working days of our shops are reduced from twelve in the fortnight to ten or nine or eight – no wonder Chichester is dull!

He refers to there being a large number of good houses in the main streets, and the drawbacks the householders suffered as a result of the market:

> But the occupants of these houses cannot drive up to them for the sheep and pigs in their pens … moreover the houses are disturbed in the early morn by the arrival of the animals for sale, and by the talk that follows in the streets: invalids cannot live in them: the smell is described at times as suffocating.

He also exposes the plight of shoppers:

> Since this was in print I have heard of the ladies of two wealthy farmers who would come to Chichester for their shopping on Market day if they could have access to the shops and then drive home with their husbands. As it is impossible, and, as they must use the train, they prefer Brighton.

Then comes the rallying cry:

> I put it therefore to my fellow-citizens, whether they will long permit the Cattle Market to depreciate their property, to injure their trade and to affect the character of their City? Let it be removed without the City, and let our council at once commence the process. We are told the land is ready; but we are told too that we, the dissatisfied, must make the move. *We have made the move …*

There was much more than a grain of truth in Swainson's criticism of the mayor and corporation. In November of that year another petition, this time signed by 92 citizens and led by Mr Dilke, was delivered to the mayor and corporation, complaining about the lack of action since their previous representation in 1864 and stating that they 'respectfully desire to be informed what measures you are willing to take in the matter, as the continued increase of the market brings with it a corresponding increase of the evils complained of'.

A way out of the woods

Although the minutes (perhaps unsurprisingly) make no mention of Swanson's pamphlet, the corporation had obviously been stung by all that had been happening, and a special council meeting was called for 20 November 1866. At this meeting the petitions were again read out and a momentous resolution, moved by Alderman William Johnson and seconded by Alderman C.T. Halsted, was passed: 'It is unanimously resolved that it is expedient for the sake of convenience that the Market held in the streets be removed to a more commodious quarter.'

Momentous though this resolution was, nothing was to happen quickly, but the need for an Act of Parliament to build the market – and to find a suitable site for it – was identified. In January 1867 the lengthy report of

21 *A rather faded view of the beast market in East Street on the last day of trading, 26 April 1871. Sheep are penned on the south side of the street, and the degree to which access to the shops was obstructed can be appreciated. The building in the foreground is the Chichester Bank.*

an inquiry held on 26 and 27 October 1866 under the Sanitary Act of that year was published and, as might be expected, it was damning about the fact that a city with a population of 8,000 souls should have no water supply or drainage and was still holding a beast market in the streets. Mr Dilke wrote again to the mayor in June 1867 accusing him of having taken no action, and another special meeting was set up for 22 October to discuss the removal of the market. What happened next rightfully belongs to the (new) Cattle Market story and will be told in Chapter Eight, but it was obvious from a letter from the Dean and Chapter read to the meeting that even at this late stage, despite the mountain of opposition, the corporation were still intent on extending the market into West Street. Their arrogance is staggering.

22 *A view of the beast market in North Street on the last day of street trading, 26 April 1871. This clearly shows the wattles used to pen the animals, those nearest the camera containing calves. Once again the resultant filth is much in evidence. This is a particularly interesting view as it shows, this side of the advertisement for hair cutting painted on the end of 81 North Street, the 1808 Market House still in its single-storey condition. The cart turning into East Street appears to be loaded with fleeces.*

The majesty of the law again caught up with those arrogant City Fathers in 1869 when the meeting of 29 April was occupied with the business of responding to another stern letter received from the medical department of the Privy Council, this time regarding the lack of progress made since 1865 in improving the sanitary conditions in the city. The deliberations, copies of the letter and the corporation's reply occupy 18 pages in the minute book![66]

The new Cattle Market was completed in the spring of 1871. A notice was placed in the *West Sussex Gazette* by the corporation that it would open on Wednesday 10 May and that the existing market would be thenceforward be discontinued.[67]

The last beast market in the streets was held on 26 April that year, as was reported by the *West Sussex Gazette*:

23 *Order returns to East Street: an Edwardian postcard view from roughly the same viewpoint as Gilbert's painting (see Fig. 16) but without the mess and chaos of the beast market. Now it was all banking and shopping in this street.*

> The cattle market was held for the last time in the streets of the city on Wednesday week, and the old posts which stood in the East Street where the bullock market was held have been removed. Some time must necessarily elapse ere it will be known how the change will affect the general interests of the City, but it must be the wish of all that the new market will grow and prosper …

The same issue contained a lengthy, and rather pompous, article written by 'Eye Witness' entitled 'Chichester Market – In Memoriam', in which he gives his memories of the beast market in the streets and then goes on to bemoan the increase in tolls at the new market and predicts that it would encourage home sales by farmers. How wrong he was to be![68]

Although he was to live to see the creation of this proper cattle market, the crusading Canon Swainson unfortunately died before his other wish was to be fulfilled. The provision of a sewerage system did not take place until 1889 – and then only after several outbreaks of cholera, emanating from the waters of the heavily polluted River Lavant, had caused deaths in the city and persuaded the corporation to remove their collective heads from the sand.

FOUR

The Market House (The Butter Market)

As we saw in Chapter Three, Chichester Common Council, at their meeting on 17 December 1802, debated the future form of all the Chichester markets, but the resolution they took pertained particularly to the general markets:

> At this Assembly it is proposed and unanimously agreed that as the holding of the Market in different parts of the City is extremely inconvenient as well to the inhabitants as to the persons exposing Articles of food for sale, and as it would be very desirable to establish a Market in some fixed place, a Committee of this Body consisting of the Mayor, Mr Alderman Drew [and several others] be appointed to seek for some spot within the Walls which may be adopted for the purpose and if necessary, to have Estimates made of the probable expenses attending the Measure to lay before the Body at some future meeting. And be it further agreed that all costs which the Committee may be at this Occasion paid for out of the funds of this body.[69]

In other words, they had at last appreciated the need for the scattered market stalls to be taken off the streets and brought together. This was to lead to the building of a new market house in North Street, the building that later – and quite erroneously – became known as the Butter Market. We will explore this spurious appellation at the end of this chapter.

The special committee was empowered the following April to procure plans and estimates for a new market house, but was not permitted to enter into any 'treaty' (i.e. contract) until they had reported back to the Common Council 'at some future meeting'. As was the way with corporation business, it was some time before the special committee made their report, and they did not do so until the meeting of 13 March 1804. The estimate they presented (whose magnitude is not recorded) obviously exceeded expectations, and so it was resolved that 'the measure, tho' desirable in itself must for the present be abandoned'. Abandoned it remained for two years until the meeting of 3 April 1806, when two dwelling houses on the east side of North Street, next to the rear entrance to the *Swan* inn, were offered to the corporation for the sum of £650 by William Humphry* as a possible site for the new market house. This offer was enthusiastically accepted, the treasurer was ordered to pay a £100 deposit immediately and the committee set about preparing an agreement for the purchase of the buildings and securing their demolition.[70]

A bill was put before Parliament resulting in the Act we encountered in Chapter Three, an Act that permitted the corporation to regulate the Cattle Market and also build the new Market House.[71] The bill did not get enacted until 8 August 1807, by which time construction was well underway, but fortunately no one seems to have noticed this unlawful anticipation of the will of Parliament!

Instead of raising the money by public subscription, as had been the case for the Council House and Assembly Rooms, the Act required the corporation to seek investors in the project who would be granted annuities for life. The annuities were to be paid quarterly out of the tolls received, and the Act provided the wording to be used for the individual forms of grant between the investor and the council. John Marsh was usually an enthusiastic supporter of public causes, but strangely the Market House seems not to have attracted his attention; he did not invest and makes no comment upon it in his journals until its opening.

A new Market House

The architect chosen was the celebrated John Nash (1752-1835), who was surveyor general to the Prince Regent, for whom he was later to remodel the Royal Pavilion along the coast in Brighton. Nash promptly prepared a design that was considered at the Common Council meeting of 4 August 1806.[72] It was duly approved, and a committee was set up to invite tenders and seek advances from those willing to invest in the project; a ceiling of £2,000 being set.[73] On 9 March 1807 an invitation to submit tenders was published in the *Hampshire Telegraph* and the contract was awarded on 17 April 1807 jointly to local builders William Brooks and Thomas Cobden in the sum of £1,522 0s. 0d.[74]

Nash's design was for a single-storey building with a hexastyle Roman Doric portico, behind which was a main hall of timber construction with 14 booths, marked as 'shops', housed in aisles, seven down each side, the cross-section drawing indicating cellars below those on the north side. The main floor area was left clear for the erection of free-standing stalls

---

* William Humphry was, as it happens, an alderman *and* a member of the brewing family who owned the *Swan*, so there is a hint of insider dealing going on here.

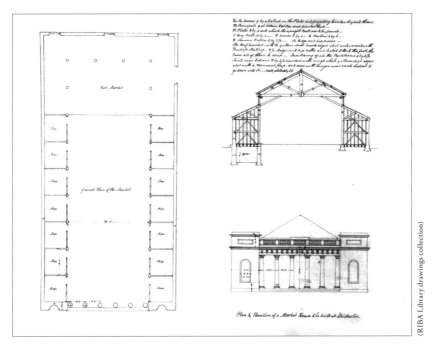

(RIBA Library drawings collection)

24 *One of Nash's drawings for the Market House, which shows the layout of the 'shops' in aisles with an open area for fish at the back. The cross-section shows that the building was a single-storey timber hall.*

or shambles. The building was approached by two wide stone steps up from the pavement, and at night could be secured by pairs of iron gates hung from the columns. At the east end, beyond the main hall, there was an area for a fish market, which was open to the sky in the interest of dispersing piscatorial odours, although there were canopies around the walls to protect the stall-holders from the worst of the elements. There appears to have been a partition wall between the main hall and the fish market to prevent the same odours pervading the rest of the building. The columns and balustrade of the portico were of Portland stone, but the flanking wings were built in brick and rendered in Parker's cement, coloured and 'jointed' (i.e. scored) to imitate Portland stone.

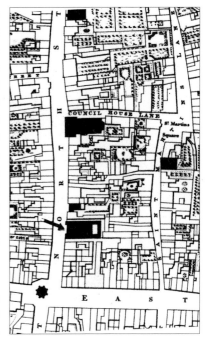

25 *An extract from Fuller's town plan of 1820 showing the Market House (arrowed) on the east side of North Street. The hole in the shading indicates the open fish market at the rear.*

The council minutes include nothing by way of progress reports on the works, and it is not until the meeting of 14 January 1808 that we learn that the building was complete, since it was resolved that the following notice be placed in the Sussex and Hampshire papers, advertising the fact that the Market House would open for business on 20 January:[75]

> Whereas the Market House in the North Street of the City of Chichester And the Stands Stalls Sheds Shambles and other Conveniences within such Market House are Now built and completed, Notice is Hereby Given that such Market House will be opened on Wednesday the 20th day of this Instant January and that on that day And on all Market Days from thenceforth the several Tolls or Sums of Money inscribed on a Table and set up in the same Market House will be imposed and taken according to the Directions of an Act Passed in the 47th Year of His present Majesty's Reign ...
>
> By Order of the Mayor, Aldermen and Citizens of the said City of Chichester
>
> JOHNSON Town Clerk
> Jany 14th 1808

There does not seem to have been an opening ceremony, so the first day must have been decidedly low key,* but the correspondent of the *Brighton Herald* was suitably impressed – as reflected in his report in the issue of 23 January 1808 :

> On Wednesday the new market house was opened for the reception of the usual articles and was fully attended by buyers and sellers. There was an excellent shew of butcher's meat. In conformity to an act of parliament obtained for the purpose, it is to be a toll market. The various stalls have let at prices sufficient to pay the interest of the money expended in the erection of this handsome structure which is of the Doric order, and does the architects† Messrs Brook and Cobden great credit. The Cross, in which the market was formerly held, will now be enclosed with railings, so there is no truth in the report that it is now to be removed. It is in contemplation to purchase the row of houses to the north side as far as the Dolphin Inn, this would certainly be desirable, as it would place this elegant specimen of Gothic architecture in a better point of view. Goths indeed must they be who would even harbour the idea of destroying so fine a piece of antiquity. We shudder at it!!

James Dallaway, in his 1815 *History of Western Sussex*, describes the new Market House as being 'a considerable embellishment' to North Street

---

* Marsh records in his diary for that day that the new market house was opened and that it had been 'about 5 months building'.

† The mis-attribution of Nash's design to the builders is a little unfortunate.

26 *A 19th-century engraving of the Market House as built. It looks unfamiliar to today's eyes as the building is now of two storeys, a result of the rebuilding that took place in 1900. The portico is surmounted by a version of the city arms made of Coade stone.*

but attributes the design to one 'T. Nash', an error that unfortunately was picked up and perpetrated by later authors.[76]

Railings were indeed installed at the cross, as can be seen in Fig. 27, which also shows that the buildings of the north side had indeed been demolished, as the *Brighton Herald* reporter predicted. However, this last action, taken in 1810, was in the interests of improving the traffic flow around the cross, not improving the view of it.

The Act required the corporation to provide a weighing house, to keep 'good and sufficient standard weights and scales, steelyards and measures', and to levy tolls against a table of 43 specified headings. The magnitude of the tolls was also dictated and these varied according to the quantities sold.

The commodities listed are butter, poultry (including fowls, chicken and ducks), wild fowl, rabbits, turkeys, geese, pigeons' eggs, fish, lobsters, crawfish, crabs, prawns, shrimps, cockles, mussels, fruit, vegetables, roots ('viz potatoes, turnips, carrots, parsnips and onions'), live or dead sucking pigs, dead hogs and porkers and fresh pork. Strangely there was no mention of beef or mutton, and it was most noticeable that no provision had been made in the Act for the corn market – indeed it made the holding of any market outside the Market House unlawful except for the beast and corn markets.

In addition to the merchandise the table set out charges relating to the stalls themselves:

	s.	d.
For every Stall or Shed, used by a Butcher for selling Flesh, being actually his own Property, per Day	1	0
For every Stall or Shed, used by a Person for exposing to Sale Cheese, Bacon, or Pickled Pork, per Day	1	0
And every person having any Article or Thing which is not included in this Table, or for selling any Article or Thing for which he can claim a legal Exemption from the Toll to pay for such Stall or Shed, per day	1	0

27 *An engraving of the Market Cross, c.1810, when it had been enclosed with railings and the buildings on the north-east corner demolished to make way for road widening.*

These entries are interesting, as they suggest that it was expected that some traders would bring their own stalls or sheds into the Market House instead of using those provided by the corporation, although this offered no pecuniary advantage. It is not clear from this how the fixed booths in the aisles, indicated as 'shops' on Nash's drawings, were intended to be used – or at what cost. The Act also gave the corporation powers to establish rules and bylaws for the conduct of the market, and to amend these 'from time to time' as necessary.

In business

What did not get reported in the press is that, in addition to making the Market Cross redundant, the opening of the Market House also brought about the demise

28 *A set of scales from the Market House, provided in accordance with the Act and now in the collection of Chichester District Museum.*

of the fish shambles in South Street, the meat market under the Assembly Rooms and individual market stalls elsewhere in the streets.

The complicated business of calculating and collecting the tolls was carried out by corporation employees at the start, but at the council meeting of 5 July 1822 it was resolved, using the powers of the Act, to lease collection of the Market House tolls by auction for a period of only one year, presumably as an experiment. As with the beast market tolls the successful bidder would pay an annual fixed sum to the corporation and in return would collect and pocket the tolls, chase defaulting payers and hope to make a profit. The successful bidder was a Mr Boniface, who tendered £265 for the privilege, and this was renewed without tender the following Michaelmas for the reduced figure of £210.[77] When the tolls again came up for auction in 1831 the conditions were altered to allow the corporation exclusive use of the Market House during elections, and Stephen Luke,

29 *The table of tolls made for display in the Market House and now in the collection of Chichester District Museum.*

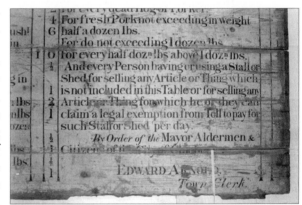

30 *A detail of the table of tolls.*

the man who won the job of collector of tolls under these conditions, was awarded £1 to compensate him for his losses during one such election in 1835.[78]

A fairly quiet existence

For most of the early Victorian era the Market House seems to have led a relatively trouble-free existence, for it does not take up much of the Common Council's time at their meetings. Indeed, apart from running repairs it is only the business of the tolls that concerns them, day-to-day matters being dealt with by various committees whose business, from 1867, is recorded in separate minute books.[79] Mr Luke gave up his duties in 1837 owing to ill health, and upon re-tender the Market House tolls were let to Henry Farr for £190 a year; curiously his was not the highest bid since Thomas Combes came in with £200. The reason for this award, which was seemingly not in the citizens' best interest, was withheld from the minutes. There did not seem to be any fear of auditors in those days![80]

When the lease for the tolls again expired in 1855 the corporation decided not to invite new tenders but to receive the tolls themselves, and the job of collection was given to James Martin, one of the city sergeants, for an extra 12s. per week. Maybe the income dropped as result of this methodology, or Mr Martin was just not very good at his job; either way in April 1857 it was decided to go back to the previous arrangement of leasing the tolls and James Bridger won the honour, bidding £90 a year.[81] It is noticeable that successive tenders had been getting progressively lower, but Bridger's bid was substantially lower than for previous years; possibly as he had also been collector of the beast market tolls since 1850 he was able to offer a better deal. Indeed, in 1866 his tender had dropped to £70.

At this time, of course, the vigorous public opposition to the beast market was occupying most of the Common Council's time, but the Market House managed to give rise to a bit of commotion over a most unexpected issue – a urinal. At their meeting of 19 June 1863 it was resolved to install a urinal in the south-west corner of the Market House, supplied with water by a pump. Plans were drawn up and estimates were sought. This was a facility that, it would be imagined, would be positively welcomed by traders and buyers alike, but how wrong could they have been? The following month the mayor received a petition from '60 inhabitants' urging the council to rescind the resolution. We are not told the reason for this mass objection (could this have been Victorian modesty?), but the petition was sufficient to stop the succinctly named Urinal Committee in its tracks, and find instead an alternative site round the corner in Lion Street.[82] A urinal was later provided in the Market House but it was set to be a constant source of complaints.

Another unexpected imbroglio arose in 1869 when a proposal was put to the council to remove from the Market Cross the railings that had enclosed it since the Market House opened in 1808. This was floated at the meeting of 8 July, but 11 days later a special meeting was called at the behest of Cllr Molesworth and four others to debate the issue. It appeared that news of the proposal had not been met with universal acclaim by the citizenry, and the mayor had received petitions both for and against the removal. It seems that some saw the cross becoming a haunt of undesirables if left open. At the meeting Aldermen Collins and Halsted proposed removal, but after the petitions had been read out Cllr Molesworth proposed that the motion be rescinded – which it was on a vote of nine to six. The railings were set to remain for a while longer, with the Market Cross continuing to be an inaccessible ornament in the middle of the city.

The Market House met with the censure of the medical officer, F.J. Freeland, in 1878. He submitted a report to the Common Council on some unpleasant findings:

> The North Street Market might be better kept both as regards the area and byplaces [*sic*]. Complaints have been frequently made with reference to watering the streets and to the state of the surface which, when frequently unavoidably disturbed is left unsightly and even dangerous condition.
>
> There is irregularity in removing refuse from the courts. The urinal is occasionally neglected and great complaints have been made of it as a nuisance to the neighbourhood: this subject has been thoroughly considered before. I believe I may say with the result of a general consensus of opinion that it would be difficult to find another place with fewer objections. A gentleman who has been a prominent objector purchased his property with this evil in its present proportions.[83]

By 1880 the problems had spread to the fabric, for in September that year the surveyor was ordered to report on the various states of the tables 'in the fish market', the place for the disposition (*sic*) of refuse and the windows. What he found was obviously serious, for in December a contract was let to Sidney Rogers to the tune of £105 6s. 2d. for the necessary repairs. Thereafter the surveyor was ordered to inspect the building regularly 'with a view to its being kept in good order in future'.[84] The 'prominent objector' who is unnamed in the medical officer's report was probably Mr W. Fogden, who makes vociferous complaints in 1894 about the urinal and an overflow of the Market House cesspit.[85]

A change of direction

From 1888 the fortunes of the Market House began to occupy much more of the Common Council's time than hitherto, as things were not going too well. In February that year it was resolved by the Common Council to use its powers under the 1807 Act to amend the bylaws, so as to close the market at 10.30 p.m. on Saturdays instead of 11 p.m. and make some other stipulations, including:

> Sellers shall only use stalls, sheds or standings as directed or ordered
> No smoking or disorderly behaviour
> No selling on the street, pavement or steps
> All persons using the market to obey lawful orders by the Mayor, Surveyor or Lessee

The resolution ended with the statement that defaulters would be punished under the penalties contained in the Act. We can infer from this that the conduct of the market was leaving much to be desired; some sellers were evading the tolls by trading outside and income was doubtless falling off as a result.[86]

Those measures do not seem to have improved matters, for in 1896 a series of decisions was taken by the Common Council that would change the appearance and layout of the Market House completely. The Finance Committee held a special meeting on 22 June 1896, which resulted in a resolution to request the General Purposes Committee to 'take into their serious consideration' closing the Market House and either using the site for other municipal purposes or disposing of it. Failing either of these outcomes, the tolls and their means of collection should be 'reconsidered'. The Market House was obviously still not paying its way, and it seemed as though its days might be numbered. In January 1897 it was resolved to revoke the council's bylaws under the Act subject to its being confirmed by the Local Government Board, but this revocation actually involved the compilation of a new set of bylaws rather than throwing everything out of the window, as the minute seems to imply.

As no copy of the original bylaws has survived it is interesting to take a look at these new ones. They comprise eight pages of very verbose legalese under 15 headings. The first gives the purpose (see Fig. 31) but the remainder can be summarised as follows:

Persons selling must only use the parts of the market house so appropriated.

No smoking, no obstruction of passages, no noisy, riotous or disorderly behaviour.

No goods to be brought in before 5 a.m.

No goods to remain after 11 p.m.

No selling in the street, on the pavement or upon the steps ('any fish, vegetables, goods or articles whatsoever').

Occupiers not to allow their goods to project beyond the line of their stalls.

Occupiers not to block passageways with receptacles for carrying goods 'for any longer than reasonably necessary'.

Occupiers to cleanse their stalls immediately before reception of goods and immediately after selling.

Occupiers to place all 'filth, garbage and refuse' in receptacles provided either by the Town Council or by themselves so as not to cause a nuisance.

BYE-LAWS

MADE BY THE MAYOR, ALDERMEN AND CITIZENS OF THE CITY OF CHICHESTER, ACTING BY THE COUNCIL,

WITH RESPECT TO

THE MARKET AT

THE MARKET HOUSE,

IN THE NORTH STREET, IN THE CITY OF CHICHESTER.

INTERPRETATION.

1. Throughout these bye-laws the expression "The Town Council" means the Mayor, Aldermen and Citizens of the City of Chichester, acting by the Council.

For regulating the use of the market house and the buildings, stalls, pens, and standings therein, and for preventing nuisances or obstructions therein, or in the immediate approaches thereto.

2. A person resorting to the market house for the sale of any goods, provisions, marketable commodities or articles shall not, for the purpose of sale or of exposure for sale, place or cause to be placed such goods, provisions, marketable commodities or articles in any part or parts of the market house other than such as shall have been appropriated for the reception, deposit, or exposure for sale of the

31 *The title page of the 1897 bylaws for the Market House. Although by this time the term Butter Market was passing into common usage, the corporation stuck to the proper title for legislative purposes.*

32 *An early 20th-century view of the Market House following the rebuilding. Only the portico remains of Nash's work; everything behind it is new.*

No vehicles or beasts of burden to stand in passageways for longer
than reasonably necessary for loading and unloading.

'All vegetable or animal refuse, filth, litter or rubbish' arising from
loading and unloading operations to be removed 'as often as
occasion may require'.

No goods to obstruct the passage of persons or vehicles through the
Market House.

Market to be open from 7 a.m. to 8 p.m. Monday to Friday, 7 a.m.
to 10.30 p.m. Saturday and closed all day Sunday.

All offenders liable to a penalty of £5 for 'offending against' the bylaws.

The bylaws were given under the common seal of the City of Chichester
and signed by the mayor, Adolphus Ballard, and the town clerk on
22 January 1897, and they received the assent of the Local Government
Board on 26 April following.

From this it can be seen that the bylaws had nothing to do with the
status quo of the Market House as stipulated by the Act (it was still a toll
market), but merely the way in which tenants and occupiers must conduct
themselves – and when.[87]

Salvation from closure came in the unlikely form of the Chichester
Technical Institute. This body was housed in premises in Crane Street that
were becoming too small, and at their meeting of 23 September 1898 the
Common Council resolved to adopt a proposal that had been laid before
them by the Technical Institute Committee, namely to seek tenders for
the building of an art school and technical institute 'to a design now laid
before the council'.[88]

The design in question had come from the city surveyor, James Saunders, and was for rebuilding the Market House so as to provide an upper floor to house the institute. Approval having been given, contracts were let in May 1899 to Messrs C. Hooker for the building works (£1,886) and Messrs Measures Bros for the supply of ironwork (£170).[89]

The work carried out to house the Technical Institute was drastic. Francis Steer, in his Chichester Paper on the Market House, made the mistake of saying that an extra floor was added for this purpose, but this was rather wide of the mark. What actually happened was that Nash's timber market hall was swept away completely, and behind the portico a new two-storey building was provided. The upper floor was carried on riveted wrought-iron girders intermediately supported by a row of five cast-iron columns. The ground floor was left for the general market but its whole area was now enclosed, the former fish market at the rear having been subsumed by the new building. A new public urinal was provided in the south-west corner, which was accessible from North Street when the market was closed via a separate entrance off Swan Lane.

Work commenced in 1899 and the opening date for the Technical Institute by the mayor was set for 24 May 1900. As with the best construction projects there was an overspend, and the final account presented to the Finance Committee in May 1900 was for £2,391 15s. 6d., but this was seemingly accepted without demur.[90]

The retention of Nash's portico was fortunate, and to make it look more at home the North Street elevation of the new upper floor was given a classical treatment in Portland stone to match. Above the six Doric columns of the portico six Ionic pilasters were provided in the correct Classical ascendancy, and at either side two projecting wings with round-headed windows reflected the niches below.

Of the niches in the original wings, the northern one was converted into a doorway providing access to the stairs leading to the upper floor, while a drinking fountain was inserted into the southern one. This drinking fountain was the gift of Alderman Adolphus Ballard, Mayor of Chichester

33 *Alderman Ballard, the generous donor of the drinking fountain, pictured when he was Mayor of Chichester and the fate of the Market House hung in the balance. He owned an ironmongery business in East Street that backed onto the Market House, and in 1896 published a history of Chichester.*

in 1896-7, who wished an inscription to be provided connecting his gift with the queen's diamond jubilee. As the said jubilee had occurred in 1897 this particular tribute was running rather late; Her Majesty would doubtless not have been amused by the alderman's tardiness. Inscriptions were added to the frieze of the wings of the portico in Parker's cement: 'Technical Institute' above the entrance to the upper floor and 'Diamond Jubilee Memorial' above the alderman's drinking fountain.

As built, the new façade and the portico below it must have married quite well, and at first sight looked as though they had always been together. The effect was later spoiled when the portico was painted in cream (Nash's favourite treatment for his stuccoed buildings, but not actually specified for this particular one), but the upper floor was not, so now the two halves sit in slightly uncomfortable juxtaposition. The other three external elevations of the new building were less elegant: they were in red brick with iron-framed windows, imparting something of an industrial air.

In May 1900 a notice was attached to the front of the rebuilt Market House inviting applications to rent the stalls inside. A few applications were received, Mrs Barnes and Mr Roberts being the first traders on the new floor, but there was hardly a flood and so it was resolved to partition off the east end of the market floor for temporary use as a workshop until such times as business picked up. At the same time the town clerk was requested by the Finance, Parliamentary, Railway and General Purposes Committee (under which body the affairs of the general market were now managed) to investigate whether street hawking could be let or licensed under the terms of the 1807 Act. This suggests that unlawful street trading was becoming commonplace and so, if the traders could not be enticed into the Market House, the corporation would try to charge them for the privilege of selling outside it. As the Act specifically outlawed street trading it is not surprising that the town clerk's answer was an emphatic 'no'.[91] The problem obviously worsened, for four years later Mr Beatson, the caretaker-cum-toll collector, was ordered to prosecute those he found selling goods in the street under the terms of the Act.

There were 44 stalls on the trading floor, and the scale of charges set in 1904 was determined on their position relative to the street. The seven in the front came at 6d. a day, the intermediate 12 at 5d. a day, while the 25 in the murky recesses of the back were only 4d. a day.[92]

The Market House, having escaped threatened closure some 20 years earlier, was still not being fully utilised, and so in August 1919 the Finance, Parliamentary, Railway and General Purposes Committee placed a new notice on the front of the building, advising the public that 'the Butter Market [sic] is available for the sale of produce by small holders, and others, in small quantities'.

Meanwhile Councillors Fowler and Hobbs were appointed as a sub-committee to investigate the state of the building and to 'act as they may consider advisable'. What they found was not promising: in direct contravention of the bylaws the stall-holders were leaving behind their refuse, and the rotting fish and produce was, not unreasonably, giving rise to complaints of smells. This olfactory assault was obviously most noticeable in the summer and resulted, in August 1920, in a copy of the said bylaws being displayed in the Market House, stall-holders being threatened with legal proceedings if they continued to transgress. A year later the threats had not worked, and so the intriguingly named Inspector of Nuisance was ordered to serve notice on the offenders ordering them to remove their refuse daily. This too had absolutely no effect, and so in 1925 the Sanitary, Drainage and Waterworks Committee instructed the town clerk to write to the fish and fruit stall-holders, informing them that as no notice had been taken of the inspector's letters the committee was 'contemplating taking severe action and that they run the risk of losing their stalls'. Desperate measures indeed. The lavatorial arrangements in the Market House were also giving rise to complaints, and the city surveyor was constantly producing schemes for improvements. All in all the 1920s were not a golden age of marketing, and a visit to the Market House at this time seems not to have been an altogether pleasant experience.[93]

The sub-committee reconvened once again to bring about a reordering of the market floor to provide fixed fish stalls, with proper slabs, at the east end and renewal and repositioning of the others. The long-suffering city surveyor designed the new layout, which was approved on 11 September 1929. The existing stall-holders were 'interviewed' about the reorganisation and the new rates, and told that any who refused to accept the new terms would be given notice to quit.[94] Such was the caring attitude of the corporation towards its tenants!

In the doldrums

Despite the reordering of the stalls, the 1930s did not usher in a marked improvement in the buoyancy of the general market; indeed it seemed to have entered the doldrums. As more and more of the floor area of the Market House became unused, it acquired a

34 *The Market House, c.1940. To the left is the entrance to the Technical Institute, which had been joined by the public library in 1932. To the right is Alderman Ballard's drinking fountain, whose dedication is recorded in the frieze above. Inside the portico the glazed tiled wall of the troublesome urinal can be seen.*

somewhat unsavoury air, as depicted in a contemporary account penned in 1935 by Tony Catton:

> A link with the period when the market was held in this street is provided by the 'Butter Market', a dreary, grey, untidy, classical building. Once, I suppose, it was fresh and clean, but nowadays it seems as if it could never have been used for the sale of butter, it is so dirty and frowzy. The central hall is a filthy, drab, smelly place, with two or three fish and fruit stalls. On Saturday nights it is the haunt of 'cheap jacks' and purveyors of artificial stockings. It is an interesting experience to attend one of these auctions. The sly vendor, uttering his coarse jokes and encouraging the shouting and laughing crowd, the drunken men and the coarse, weary-faced women form a strange picture which, if the characters were dressed in 18th-century costume, might well have been taken from one of Hogarth's drawings. In the upper storey of the 'Butter Market' is housed the public library and is the nucleus of a small museum, which is being formed in the town.[95]

Tony Catton was only 15 when he wrote this. It comes from a 'brief history of Chichester' written for his friend Charles Kimbell who was emigrating to Australia. His research and prose style reveal a wisdom way beyond his years, but tragically he was killed during the Second World War before reaching his prime.

The portico was partly painted in 1935, and that same year the bylaws were revised again – but were incorporated with those of the Cattle Market at the recommendation of the Ministry of Health.[96] Unfortunately it has not been possible to trace a copy of these bylaws so we cannot gauge the changes and what they were intended to achieve. Business was so slack that in 1939, just after the outbreak of the Second World War, the Finance Committee could not grant the Women's Institute, who had set up their stall on 1 April 1938, a reduction in rent from 12s. 6d. to 7s. 6d., but three years earlier the Left Book Club's application to open a stall, which would have brought in new business, had been refused. Seemingly that type of business was not welcome in true-blue Chichester.

The Second World War saw three opportunistic bombing raids on Chichester, one of which took place in daylight on 10 February 1943. The first bomb exploded in Chapel Street where, in addition to flattening a number of cottages, it destroyed the premises of Mr R.R.W. Stringer, a tent contractor at no. 25. The city's emergency committee resolved to allow Mr Stringer temporary use of the rear part of the under-used Market House in order to re-establish his business at the weekly rent of £6. Unfortunately Mr Stringer's stay proved to be anything but temporary – or happy. He only began to consider rebuilding his Chapel Street premises in 1949, and from October 1951 he omitted to pay his rent. By July 1953 he owed the council £525 16s. in rent arrears, and so the county sheriff seized his goods to this value. Mr Stringer was finally evicted from the Market House the following October.[97]

After the war the fortunes of the Market House continued to spiral downwards, and the provisions of the 1807 Act were perceived to be part of the problem so the town clerk was instructed to consult parliamentary agents about modernising the corporation's powers thereunder, particularly in respect of the list of tolls. From this we infer that the original tolls, now considerably devalued by inflation, were still being charged. In April 1948 the town clerk submitted a memo (now lost) with recommendations for the alterations to the Act which were duly approved by the Markets Committee.

This resulted in a parliamentary bill for a provisional order that would, *inter alia*, repeal two clauses and alter others in the 1807 Act so as to allow the corporation to introduce new tolls, alter the places in which markets were held, discontinue, alter or enlarge existing markets, grant leases and use part of the Cattle Market for a general market. The bill also included provisions in respect of the running of the Cattle Market; but most importantly for the Market House it sought powers to 'provide shops, catering establishments, offices and other buildings in connection with the market'. A public inquiry was called for Tuesday 8 February 1949 at the council offices under Mr V.D. Joll BSc AMICE, an engineering inspector of the Ministry of Health.[98]

The inquiry was duly held, and in its report under the headline 'Threat of cheap-jack invasion' the *Chichester Observer* reported that the Chichester Chamber of Trade had objected to the clauses that would allow the setting up of stalls in the Cattle Market on the grounds that it would result in a lowering of the standard of trading in the city, their solicitor saying that 'it is felt that the almost universal trend is for traders making use of market stalls to consist largely of the cheap-jack type who sell inferior shoddy articles at prices below those agreed upon by the trade'. Mr Eric Banks, the town clerk, told the inquiry that the corporation desired to modernise the Market House and provide improved facilities for stall-holders so as to develop the market as a commercial enterprise. No one seems to have raised any objection to this part of the bill.[99] The provisional order received royal assent on 30 July 1949.[100]

The year 1951 saw new threats to the continued functioning of the Market House. In December the Markets Committee, under whose jurisdiction it had come since 1949, made a tripartite resolution whose purpose was to do away with the general market in North Street using the new powers:

> (a) That, in the opinion of this Committee, the present use of the building should in due course, be discontinued; (b) that the building be converted into business premises; and (c) that the City Surveyor be instructed to prepare a scheme for the erection of a covered retail market in the Cattle Market.

News of the impending availability of the Market House got out, and a number of proposals for leasing the building came before the council, but the continued presence of the Art School on the first floor proved a stumbling block, so none came to fruition.[101]

Meanwhile, others within the council had designs on the building, for in October 1952 the Finance Committee investigated a proposal to turn it into a museum and art gallery since the Guildhall, which contained the city's larger museum exhibits, was deemed inadequate for the purpose. It was proposed that Roman remains would be displayed on the ground floor with smaller items, manuscripts and pictures on the first. This last would include the Eric Gill collection that had recently been bequeathed to Chichester.[102] Nothing more is recorded about this so the idea was obviously dropped. Probably the difficulty in evicting the Art School killed it, but the proposal is an interesting 'might have been'.

In December 1953, in the wake of the unfortunate Mr Stringer's financial misfortune, the surveyor was instructed to prepare a scheme for building a new covered market on the site of Stringer's bombed-out premises on the east side of Chapel Street. The building would house 32 stalls, have access from North Street and cost an estimated £7,500. Quite why, when the existing market was not attracting business, a new one in the same street was expected to do better is puzzling, but light eventually dawned upon the committee and the idea was dropped in February 1954.

Interest in leases of the Market House continued, however, and one was submitted in June 1954 by agents Elliott, Sons and Boynton for their unnamed client who wished to remove the portico and replace it with modern shop fronts. This came to the attention of the Ministry of Housing and Local Government, who pointed out that the building was now listed* and expressed the hope that the council would find some use that did not involve alterations.[103] Fortunately the ministerial advice was heeded and Nash's portico lived on.

The 1955 revival

Despite the gloom of the previous five years a momentous decision was taken by the Markets Committee in September 1954 that the Market House would not, after all, be closed but retained for its intended purpose, remodelled and run under the new powers in the provisional order. Once again the city surveyor got busy preparing schemes that would provide vehicular rear access from St Martin's Street, new lock-up stalls of varying sizes, showcases and store rooms – and abolish the noisome urinal.

The scheme that was finally signed off by the Markets Committee on 14 February 1955 provided a total of 21 stalls, 13 stores and three showcases.

---

* It was listed Grade II* in 1950.

These were to be leased for seven years and attract a weekly rent. The distribution of the stalls and their rents was as follows:

2 large stalls	£4 10 s. per week
19 small stalls	£2 10s. per week
13 stores	10s. per week
2 small showcases	10s. per week
1 large showcase	£1 10s. per week

The revamped market was an instant success, probably because the lock-up stalls had an air of permanency that the old tables lacked and provided small traders with a proper shop at a realistic rent. Some of the previous traders returned, including Miss Cripps the fishmonger and the Women's Institute, whose stall, selling a formidable array of home-produced goods, was always busy. Other traders during the late 1950s included H. White (fruiterer), the China Box, Mrs L.C. Hewitt (fancy goods), Ward & Marsh (fruiterers), F. Emanuel (jeweller), Mrs C.E. Farthing (fruiterer) and Parker & Prior (butchers).[104]

So successful had the revamped Market House become that two more stalls were added, bringing the total to 23, in 1957. The fact that there was rear access to the building contributed to this success, as it put the market on a through route from North Street to St Martin's Street, thus bringing in an element of passing trade.

Alderman Ballard's fountain was unceremoniously removed in 1956 to enable the southern niche to be converted into a window for Hoopers the florist, who occupied the shop in the southeast corner. The city surveyor was instructed to store the fountain until a further use could be found for it. Admittedly it was not the most elegant piece of street furniture in the city – the alderman's taste being typically high Victorian – but his munificent gift never resurfaced and was rumoured to have found its way into the garden of a well-known Cicestrian. He has since died; its current whereabouts is unknown.

35 *The interior of the Market House in 1968, showing the style of lock-up stall resulting from the 1955 remodelling. The gent in the trilby hat is studying the goods on display in the window of the China Box (who are also offering a range of shopping baskets), while behind him can be seen the stalls on the south side of the market, namely Ward & Marsh and L.A. Williams the confectioner.*

The discovery in 1961 that the Market House was the work of John Nash rather than the fictitious 'T. Nash' caused Russell Purchase, who had made the discovery, to suggest to the corporation that a commemorative plaque be affixed to the portico. This was agreed to, and the city surveyor submitted estimates for two options, a simple painted board for £15 5s. and one carved from Hopton stone at £43. The Markets Committee opted for the more expensive version, and Sir Hugh Casson was asked to suggest a suitable site for the plaque. At this time Casson* and a local architect, Vincent St Aubyn-Hubbard, were working on a civic design scheme for North Street, hence his interest. The two architects put forward a scheme in 1963 for redecorating the outside of the Market House and affixing the plaque, altogether costing £400. This involved colouring the city arms on the portico, and a dispute arose when it was found that only the shield had been so treated, with another £40 required to pick out the rest. Curiously the plaque never appeared and there is no more mention of it. Perhaps, along with the civic design scheme, the idea simply fizzled out.[105]

The so-called Butter Market was now *the* place to shop for your fish, meat, fruit and veg, and it remained a popular feature of the Chichester shopping scene for more than three decades. A proposal to extend the Market House at the rear was mooted in 1966 but fizzled out in 1968 when negotiations with adjacent property owners fell through.[106]

In 1973, when the Market House was at its zenith and a bustling place to shop, the traders and the shops they occupied were as follows:[107]

1. H. White – greengrocer
2. J. Prior – butcher
3 & 4. A.M. Cripps – fishmonger
5 & 6. Chasefair Ltd – fruiterers
7. Jackson Trading – newsagent
8. E.S. Gregory – baker
9-11. China Box – china and glass dealers
12. E.S. Gregory – baker (back to back with no. 8)
13. Central News (Jackson Trading) – newsagent
14 & 15. A. & I. Wilson – fancy goods dealer
16. Chichester & District Women's Institute
17. D.J. Griffin – antiques
18 & 19. Ward & Marsh Ltd – fruiterers
20. L.A. Williams – confectioner
21. Regnum Nurseries – florists (formerly Hoopers)
22 & 23. D. Vinall – wool store
24. Mr & Mrs Powell – antiques

---

* Sir Hugh Casson later made his mark on Chichester when he designed the replacement building for Lennard's shoe shop on the corner of North and East Streets. The building is now occupied by Gold Arts.

It can be seen that another stall had somehow been squeezed in. Some of the traders were characters, particularly Mr White, who ran his greengrocery stall with his wife and engaged in lively back-chat with his customers, all of whom he knew by name. My mother would have never dreamt of buying her greengrocery from anybody else.

And so the market continued through the 1970s and '80s, but come the 1990s supermarkets had changed people's shopping habits: the idea of being able to buy everything under one roof and then take it all home by car was proving too irresistible for many. Although the WI and the China Box remained, the supermarket effect reduced the demand for fresh produce, and so such traders departed. A new arrival in 1994 was O'Hagan's Sausages, selling a wide and exotic range of sausages that could be sampled before buying – the heady aroma wafting seductively out into North Street. Chichester School of Art had merged with Chichester College of Further Education in 1964, but remained on the top floor of the Market House. When it eventually moved to the main campus the vacant upper floor became another trading area, but for clothing and haberdashery rather than produce.

Under the local government reorganisation of 1974 Chichester City Council was reduced to parish council status, with most of its powers transferring to the new Chichester District Council, but it retained ownership and management of the Market House.

A market no more

The new millennium saw another change of direction, but this time a significant and somewhat controversial one that would see the Market House cease to be a market facility. In 2005 the city council, concerned that the building – and its roof in particular – was in need of extensive repairs and offered no disabled access to the first floor, set up a working group to investigate the options for the future of the building. They decided to carry out another major refurbishment and submitted a planning application to Chichester District Council in May 2007 for works that would retain the ethos of market stalls on both floors and provide a new staircase inside the market hall and improved facilities for the disabled. Maintaining the through-route to St Martin's Street to encourage passing trade was seen as a most important feature of the scheme, as was maintaining retail units for small businesses rather than converting the building to a single large-scale outlet.[108]

A full-page feature appeared in the *Chichester Observer* of 26 April 2007 entitled 'Why the traders <u>have</u> to leave the Butter Market', in which the town clerk explained why the refurbishment was necessary and that it could not be done with the businesses *in situ*. This sparked a revolt by

36 *Women queue at the Old City Fish Shop at the back of the Market House, January 1983. In the background can be seen the rear entrance from St Martin's Square, which generated much useful passing trade.*

the traders and their customers, who waged a campaign in the letters columns of the *Chichester Observer* that ran for several weeks. Fears expressed included that it would become more of a shopping arcade than a market, and that the rents would have to go up to fund the improvement work. A particular issue was the pending loss of the popular Women's Institute market, which had been a feature for 69 years. Despite this strength of feeling only seven people actually bothered to write to object to the planning application, but before the district council could make a decision the city council withdrew it. The reason given by their agent was that 'unexpected comments' by English Heritage on the listed building consent necessitated further consideration of the proposal.[109]

A second planning application for a slightly revised scheme was made in October 2007, and as the leases were due to expire in June that year the city council served notice on the traders to quit. This caused more outpourings of ire in the *Chichester Observer*, which reported on 5 June that the traders were very angry at having been evicted just before the busy summer period and, to make matters worse, just 11 days before the deadline they were told that the market would in fact be staying open for the time being. They were offered temporary leases to stay on, but by this time the popular O'Hagan's Sausages had already closed.[110]

The reason for the delay in closure of the Market House was that the city council had reviewed the business case, and as the cost of the refurbishment would have taken up most of their existing capital and required the financing of a loan, they decided that rather than refurbish the building themselves they would enter into a partnership agreement with a developer to take the project forward on a different footing, one that would not burden the council taxpayer.[111] Bids sought from prospective partners were reviewed in November 2007. One of the unsuccessful bidders, who proposed to retain the building as a toll market, wrote a letter to the *Chichester Observer* on 4 December 2007 attacking the city council's selection process, and a highly critical internet blog followed in March 2008.[112]

A shortlist was agreed in August 2008 from which the winner would be decided the following November.[113] The developer chosen by the city council proposed that the Market House be remodelled to provide just eight 'retail units' – four to each floor – for which a new planning application was made in December 2008, the previous one for a market having been withdrawn.[114] After being approved, a number of changes were made to the scheme as it went through the planning process, including one for replacing the gates in the portico with glass doors. This was refused and then not upheld on appeal. Interestingly the new layout did not provide for pedestrian access from the rear, a facility so much valued in the past.

Work started on site in March 2010 to provide, at ground level, fully fitted shops down each side and across the back of the former trading floor, making a feature of the central line of columns. The outer units featured curved glass ends, and at the front of the building a section of the first floor was removed to create an atrium effect. There were more shop units on the top floor. Acknowledging the building's roots, the date 1808 was incorporated in a new screen above the entrance gates, and the portico was repainted in Nash cream.

The new shopping facility was expected to open the following August or September, but by August the work was not progressing as rapidly as originally expected, and the recession in which the country found itself did not make the finding of tenants easy. The 'Butter Market' finally opened its new gates on Good Friday, 22 April 2011, and was officially opened the following day by the Mayor of Chichester, Cllr Michael Woolley. The Market House, a market no more, had begun a new life as an upmarket shopping arcade.

So whence came 'Butter Market'?

It was pointed out at the start of this chapter that the popular appellation Butter Market is entirely spurious. Exactly when the name came to be applied to the Market House became apparent during the research for this book, but any explanation for the change remains pure conjecture, as there seems to have been no reason, valid or otherwise, for the change of name.

Chichester is by no means the only city to sport a market cross (but it is the largest and finest!) and in some places these go by the name of a particular commodity, that in Salisbury for example being the Poultry Cross. A few of these structures are known as butter crosses, the one in Winchester being

37 *The hoarding that closed off the Market House for over a year from March 2010 during its redevelopment into a retail arcade.*

38 *The frontage of the Market House, August 2011. Fully fitted high street shops now occupy the space once home to market traders. It is rather suggestive of the entrance to London's Burlington Arcade. This makes an interesting comparison with Fig. 34; the former entrance to the Technical School is now a shop window and the disabled entrance has replaced Alderman Ballard's drinking fountain.*

the nearest example to Chichester. However, Chichester's market cross, as with the Market House some 300 years later, was built as a shelter for a *general* market; it never was, and has never been referred to as, a butter cross, so this cannot have been the inspiration for the renaming of the Market House.

Well into the 20th century the business of the corporation was recorded in handwritten minutes scribed directly into bound books, and from December 1867 the minutes of the various committees were recorded in their own volumes. It is in the Finance Committee's minute book, in a record of a meeting on 20 April 1872, that the term 'Butter Market' first appears, in a minute granting 'the lease of the Butter Market Tolls to Mr A.J. Bridger'.[115] From then on in the committee minutes 'Butter Market' became the almost universal term for the Market House. Could it be that whoever wrote up the Finance Committee minutes was an incomer from somewhere that had a butter cross (Winchester perhaps?) and misguidedly transferred the appellation to the Market House? Alternatively, as the new Cattle Market had opened the year before, could he have taken it upon himself to rename the Market House in an attempt to avoid (unlikely) confusion with the new facility?

In the Common (i.e. main) Council minute books each page has a wide margin on the left-hand side into which a reference, in the form of a sub-heading and brief résumé, was inserted against each minute for the benefit of future researchers. From these minutes the Common Council can be seen to have stuck to the old parlance for the building in question for six years beyond the fateful 20 April 1872, until their meeting of 9 April 1878 when the business of sealing the lease of the Market House tolls came up. While the minute itself records 'To Mr A.J. Bridger, of the tolls of the Market held in the North Street', the margin reference says 'Lease of Butter Market Tolls to Mr A.J. Bridger sealed'.[116] It is noticeable that the reference has been added in a different hand. One assumes that the Common Council minutes would have been scribed by the town clerk, but it is obvious that the references were being added later, probably by a minion. Now the handwriting in that reference is very similar to that seen in the committee books back in 1872, but I am no graphologist and I cannot swear that the same person is responsible. If he was, then he introduced his idea to the Common Council.

Those leases came up for renewal every three years, and up to 1886 in the Common Council minutes referring to them the same thing happens, the 'Butter Market' reference being added later by that same (but different) hand.[117] It is in 1888 that the damage became irreparable, for against the minute regarding the lease of tolls the reference says 'Butter Market', and is in the same hand as the minute itself. The town clerk, and therefore the Common Council, had now become infected! 'Butter Market' was passing into common currency – at least within the confines of the Council House.

The public, however, might not have been so sure, since the various Chichester directories continued to call it 'the Market House' until 1929; that year Kelly's Directory carried the wording 'here is the Butter Market'. Strangely, in its own publications the City Council seemingly could not agree upon the issue, for while their 1949 printed accounts carry an entry relating to the Butter Market their City Guide of the same year directs would-be visitors to the Market House! That same year the town clerk created legal incongruity when he placed the public notice in the *Chichester Observer* about the provisional order and referred to it as the 'Chichester Butter Market Act, 1807' instead of quoting its correct title.

Some worthies rightly stuck out for the proper name. When in 1962 Francis Steer, the revered county archivist, wrote his Chichester Paper on the subject he resolutely used the term 'Market House' throughout and never once mentioned 'Butter Market', obviously treating this historical solecism with well-deserved contempt.[118]

It is perhaps ironic that Butter Market was used as the brand name for the 2010 redevelopment since now neither 'butter' nor 'market' are applicable. However, commemorative plaques unveiled in October 2011 do use the term 'Market House'. *Sic transit*!

FIVE

A Corn Exchange for Chichester

We saw in Chapter Four how neither the new Market House in North Street nor the 1807 Act of Parliament relating to Chichester's markets made any provision for improving the lot of the corn market. Indeed the corporation seemed to have a rather cavalier attitude towards it for it hardly ever featured in their deliberations. One exception was in 1830 when on 7 May it was ordered that six members should meet 'the committee named by the growers of corn and resorting to Chichester Market and receive from them any proposals for the erection of a corn market'. They were also ordered to visit other towns to inspect their corn markets and ascertain whether they had been established by Act of Parliament or charter.[119] There is no record of the committee reporting back, emphasising their lack of interest. On the other hand those trading at the corn market do not seem to have made much effort to have their feelings heard by the powers that be, so perhaps it should not be too surprising that nothing happened.

Corn exchanges

At this time many towns conducted their corn trading in the corn exchanges that had begun to multiply across Britain from the middle of the 18th century. The City of London already had its general Royal Exchange in Cornhill, which reopened in 1671 after being destroyed in the Great Fire, but this needed to be supplemented by a separate Corn Exchange, which was built in Mark Lane. Designed by George Dance the elder,[120] it opened in 1750 and its market prices were always quoted in the national papers. Its business continued to grow and a new building, to a design by George Smith and A.B. Clayton, was built alongside in 1828. The New Corn Exchange had a rather muscular Greek Doric frontage facing onto the street that had

39 *The new City of London Corn Exchange of 1828, which has an impressive frontage of the Greek Doric order and appears to have been the model for the building at Chichester in its original form.*

all the appearances of being the work of John Soane.* The architect James Elmes, whose works in Chichester included St John's Chapel, described the new building as 'one of the most agreeable architectural compositions in the metropolis'.[121] The new London Corn Exchange provided a model for many to follow, including Chichester, but sadly it was badly damaged by enemy action in 1941 and was later demolished.[122]

Often these corn exchanges were built and run by a town's corporation, but in some cases they were private ventures with shareholders' aspirations to satisfy; but either way corn exchanges were generally imposing buildings consisting of a spacious trading hall with ample corn stores behind. Farmers brought their produce into the stores where it could remain until it was all sold. Once a week the market was held in the trading hall, and in the days following the sale buyers removed their purchases from the stores. The proprietors of corn exchanges made their money by charging tolls; firstly as

---

*   Sir John Soane (1753-1837) was a very distinguished Georgian architect who worked in the classical idiom but adapted the orders in a most individualistic manner.

the corn was received into the stores, secondly for its subsequent storage on their premises and lastly when it was removed after sale. In addition they charged a commission on each sale made.[123] Stands were rented by dealers who acted as middle-men between farmers and buyers, and on market days the prices were bargained between the dealer and the buyer – it was not an auction. It was seemingly one of those situations where everyone gained. Farmers no longer had to store grain on their farms or attend the corn market, trade was carried out under cover, proprietors made money and towns acquired versatile buildings capable of several uses. As the markets were generally only held weekly the vast trading halls were empty for the other six days, and thus were available for other purposes such as meetings, dances and theatrical performances; in towns where there were no assembly rooms this was a great boon.

The seed is sown

The blatant lack of interest in the corn market by the corporation caused farmers and corn merchants to take the matter into their own hands, and on 20 June 1832 a public meeting was called at the *Swan* inn* in East Street, chaired by James Hack, to discuss the possibility of building a corn exchange in the city. The outcome of that meeting was the following resolution, as recorded in the shareholders' minute book:[124]

40 *The Chichester Corn Exchange as originally built, in an 1833 engraving by Thomas King. The front elevation differs considerably from that which exists today, owing to a partial rebuilding that took place in 1836. To the right can be seen the* Fleece, *one of Chichester's coaching inns.*

---

*   The *Swan* was the principal coaching inn in the city and was situated on the north side of East Street, not far from the cross. It can be seen in Gilbert's view of East Street in Fig. 16. The *Swan* was a popular venue for meetings – both private and public – as well as auctions. It closed in the 1840s and the building burnt down in 1897. The Victorian Natwest bank now occupies the site.

That it is desirable that there should be a regularly established Pitched Market in the City of Chichester for the sale of Corn and Grain.

That an opportunity now presents itself of erecting the necessary Stores with other convenient Buildings on the Scite [*sic*] of certain premises in the East Street of Chichester adjoining the Cattle Market, the estimated expense of which will certainly not exceed £6000.

That such Sum be raised in shares of £25 each and that no person be allowed to subscribe his name for more than ten shares.

That the first Call on each Share be £10 and each succeeding Call £5.

That a Committee be appointed for collecting Subscriptions and making the necessary Enquiries previously to the next meeting.

That the following Gentleman do form the Committee, viz:

Mr Hack	Mr G. Henty	Mr R.B. Robins
Mr H. Freeland	Mr W. Shippam	Mr C. Duke
Mr Rusbridger	Mr T. Halsted	Mr G. Souter

of whom any five may act.

That the meeting be adjourned till Wednesday 4 July next at Six o'clock in the Evening

That the Resolution be printed and circulated with a list of the present subscribers for Shares.

James Hack, Chairman

It is noticeable that proximity to the beast market in East Street was regarded as a positive asset! The *Hampshire Telegraph* of 25 June carried an enthusiastic report of the meeting, stating that 108 shares had already been subscribed and opining that 'little doubt can be entertained of its being carried into effect'. The fact that this meeting took place against the background of an agricultural depression and the Swing Riots that had just ended in Sussex (See Chapter One), ought perhaps to have dampened the enthusiasm shown by the promoters – but seemingly it did not.

A second meeting was held on 27 June 1832 when three more committee members were appointed, namely Stephen Farndale, J.P. Hayllar and W. Field; the committee, as was to be expected, contained many well-known Chichester names. Robert Raper, a partner in the Chichester solicitors' firm of Johnson and Co.,* was appointed secretary, a post he was to occupy until his tragically early death in 1855. The local bank of Dendy, Comper and Gruggen was appointed as treasurers. The now complete committee was then charged to 'obtain Plans and Specifications and make Contracts for the Erection of the necessary Stores and proceed therein as expeditiously as possible'.

---

* This firm later, via his son Robert George Raper, became the well-known Chichester legal practice of Raper & Co., which is still in existence under the guise of Stone Milward Raper, and was operating from the same address of 55 West Street until 2009.

The shareholders' minutes contain absolutely nothing about finding the site, appointing the architect or the procurement and award of the contracts, since this information was recorded in the committee's own minute book, which, sadly, has been lost. For this vital information, and also reports on the progress of the works, we have to turn to the pages of the *Hampshire Telegraph*, a publication that, fortunately for posterity, followed the project with close interest.

In its report on the initial meeting it stated that a site had already been chosen for the Corn Exchange, namely the spacious mansion house on the south side of East Street, at its junction with Baffins Lane, that in May 1832 was up for sale following the demise of its last occupant, Mrs Fitzherbert.[125]

At a shareholders' meeting on 26 September 1832 the rules for the management of the Corn Exchange were tabled and agreed. Running to 14 printed pages, the 36 rules set out, *inter alia*, the voting rights of the shareholders, the dates for the annual general meeting, the way the company would conduct its business and, most importantly at this stage, the way in which the money to fund the building would be raised.[126]

Strangely the idea of a corn exchange does not seem to have been met with universal support, for in July a meeting had been held at the *Fleece* by supporters of the existing corn market, who appointed a committee of 24 'agriculturalists' to make resolutions about the management of the market in North Street. Opposition seemed to be mounting, supported as it was by 'upwards of 110 of the most influential corn growers and millers in the neighbourhood'. However, it all seemed to fizzle out quite quickly as there was only one more report about their activities in the *Hampshire Telegraph*, namely on 30 July, regarding a committee of 25 having been appointed to run the Northgate market.[127] One can only assume that, faced with the choice of trading in the open air or in the shelter of the grand new Corn Exchange, most of its potential clients wisely opted for the latter.

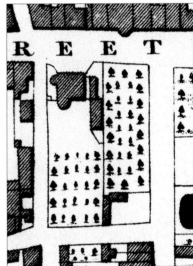

41 *An extract from George Loader's 1812 town plan showing the mansion house on the corner of East Street and Baffins Lane beneath the first 'E' of STREET. It was on the site of this house and garden that the new Corn Exchange was to be built.*

Who was the architect?

Opinion has long been divided over who designed Chichester's Corn Exchange, the two candidates, both local men, being John Elliott and George Draper. Howard Colvin, in his monumental *Dictionary*,[128] is of the opinion that the architect was Elliott, quoting as his source the Victorian *Dictionary of Architecture*, an authoritative organ published by the Architectural Publication Society. Pevsner[129] gives the same attribution but local opinion has always favoured Draper. George Draper's local architectural works included the *Swan* inn, which he rebuilt after a disastrous fire in 1819, the Chichester Infirmary of 1826 and the long drawn-out rebuilding of St Bartholomew's Church between 1824 and 1832.

The *Hampshire Telegraph* of 16 July 1832 carried the public notice inviting tenders for the work, a notice that also reveals the identity of the architect:

TO BUILDERS AND OTHERS
CHICHESTER CORN EXCHANGE

Notice is hereby given that the Committee of the CHICHESTER CORN EXCHANGE will receive tenders in writing for the Performance of the Bricklayers', Carpenters', Plumbers', Glaziers', Painters' and Slaters' WORKS in and about the intended NEW BUILDINGS; such tenders to be delivered (sealed up) to the Secretary, on or before four o'clock on Wednesday 25 July instant in the evening of which the Committee will open the same.

The Plans and Specifications will be open for inspection at the Office of the Architect, Mr Draper, St Martin's Square, Chichester on or after Wednesday next, the 18th inst.

By Order of the Committee
R. RAPER, Secretary

Since this public notice confirms that Draper was indeed the architect, how did Elliott come to be attributed with the design in the Victorian *Dictionary of Architecture*? The plot is thickened by the fact that it was actually Draper – a member of the Architectural Publication Society – who provided the entry for the Chichester Corn Exchange that named Elliott as the architect![130] The answer to this conundrum emerges from an unfortunate event that occurred two years after opening, as we shall see.

Construction

There were four contracts for the construction of the Corn Exchange, with the main contractor being Messrs Mew of Brighton.[*] The *Hampshire Telegraph* carried an intriguing report in its issue of 10 September to the effect that a rumour was being circulated about the main contractor having abandoned the works. This the correspondent roundly rebutted, saying that 'the building is now in a rapid state of progress and the Committee are perfectly satisfied with the exertions made'. One suspects that the committee of the Old Corn Market might have been responsible for spreading this malicious alarm and despondency.

---

[*] In the report on the award of the contract the *Hampshire Telegraph* gave the main contractor's name as Mew of Brighton. In this report it was given as Mellew of Brighton. Obviously one was a typographical error.

The construction obviously proceeded at a great pace, for the *Hampshire Telegraph* of 10 December, less than six months after award of contracts, carried a florid report of the topping-out ceremony, which is worth quoting in full:

> On Friday 150 persons, consisting of the workforce who have been employed in the erection of the new corn exchange in Chichester, and many gentlemen, the friends of Mr Mew, the Builder, dined together in one of the spacious storerooms of that beautiful structure which is now nearly completed. We feel pleasure in stating that Lord George Lennox honoured the meeting by his presence. The dinner, which was provided by Mr George Rees of the Golden Cross was got up in excellent order and gave universal satisfaction.

A week later the committee published a notice advising the public that the new Corn Exchange would be open for reception of corn on 20 December and would begin selling on Wednesday 2 January 1833.[131]

Despite having opened for business in December 1832, completion did not occur until the following April, so major works must have been continuing around the trading; contractors and their clients were not bound by any health and safety considerations in those far-off days, so the risk was obviously worth taking. At the annual general meeting held on 6 May 1833 the committee reported that they had exceeded the maximum authorised borrowing sum of £1,000 by £389 6s. 0d., owing to the extra expense of deeper foundations.

We are indeed fortunate that two artists captured the original appearance of the new Corn Exchange, as it assumed its present guise

42 *Another view of the Corn Exchange as constructed, this time a lithograph by Filippo Pistrucci. Although the rare print is in poor condition it gives much detail of the building that Draper provided.*

only three years later. Of the two, that of Filippo Pistrucci* given in Fig. 43 provides the most information. It was a version of this view that was used on the original share certificates.

It can be seen that the frontage of the building sat at the back of the pavement and the hexastyle Greek Doric portico, with fluted columns set *in antis* and flanked by two pavilions, gave onto an open-fronted single-storey trading hall separated from the street only by sets of gates, with its interior lit by a toplight in the clear-span roof. The frontage bears a striking resemblance to that of the 1828 London Corn Exchange (as can be judged by comparison with Fig. 40), only here the pavilions were pure Greek and framed the gateways to the access roads that ran along the east and west sides of the building. Above the pediment was a stylobate, bearing the legend 'Corn Exchange', surmounted by a castle bearing the city arms. A report in the *Hampshire Telegraph* for 4 May 1833 describes the arms as being surrounded by 'four emblems of agriculture', namely the plough, the harrow, the rake and the scythe. These are missing from Pistrucci's view but can be seen in King's in Fig. 41. Again, as this detail is so similar to the London building one has to assume that Draper had used it as a model.

The fact that Draper's frontage also loosely resembles Nash's Market House in North Street (see Fig. 26) has led many to presume that these early artists somehow got the two buildings muddled up and produced an extraordinary composite instead of an accurate representation. The similar coat of arms and castle on the Market House was supplied by Eleanor Coade of Lambeth and made of her miraculous Coade stone, but there is no entry in the firm's order book for a variant of it having been supplied for the Corn Exchange.[132]

Curiously, one of the work items outstanding when the exchange opened was the erection of the cast-iron columns (and hence the entablature above them), which did not arrive until February. They were reported as being six in number, upwards of three feet in diameter, 19 feet high and altogether weighing 18 tons 19 hundredweight.[133] They were made in horizontal sections, as was revealed when they were being prepared for repainting a few years ago, and are quite remarkable for 1833 both in the size of the castings and the way they match up perfectly at the joints.

To the rear of the trading hall was the three-storey corn store that stretched all the way back along Baffins Lane to Cross Street† in Newtown. While the trading hall facing East Street was expensively Classical, the corn store was functionally industrial in its appearance.

---

* Filippo Pistrucci was the brother of the better-known Benedetto Pistrucci, the gem engraver who produced the famous George and Dragon design used on British gold sovereigns from 1817.

† Cross Street was later renamed New Town to avoid confusion with the other Cross Street in Somerstown.

43 *The Baffins Lane corn store viewed from the south-west, 1966. At eaves level can be seen the sack hoists over the doors giving onto the storage floors. The contrast between its functionalism and the elegant stuccoed, Classical lines of the trading hall beyond is quite pronounced. The rather twee entrance porch is a much later addition.*

'Weak and injudiciously constructed'

For all the lavish praise heaped upon the completed building by the *Hampshire Telegraph* correspondent, problems soon began to manifest themselves in the form of a sagging roof to the trading hall and sagging floors in the corn store.

At an extraordinary meeting of the shareholders held on 1 August 1835,[134] the company secretary made a report that

> the building required very considerable repairs and that the Committee had taken the opinion of two or three persons as to the steps necessary to be taken from which it appeared that to put the Edifice in a complete state would require the expenditure of from four to five hundred pounds.

As the whole project, including land purchase and site clearance, had only cost £6,000 in the first place, the need to spend up to £500 to put the new building right indicates that the problems were very serious indeed.

The committee formed the opinion that Draper, the architect, should be held responsible for any loss as a consequence of any defects 'arising from want of judgement or otherwise on his part'. It was resolved to seek the opinion of learned counsel on the matter.

44 *Another view of the Baffins Lane corn store in 1966, this time from New Town and showing the eastern access road. The wall in the foreground was to the garden of Hasted House in St John's Street, which was demolished when a new house was built on the site in 2005.*

45 *An early photograph of the Corn Exchange as remodelled by John Elliott. The roofline has been extended over the pavement onto a new row of columns. Draper's side gates have been retained but of the pavilions that once framed them only the inner pilasters remain.*

Another special meeting was held on 26 August at which the secretary reported that he had procured the attendance of Mr James Savage, a London architect and civil engineer, to survey the structure of the Corn Exchange and give an opinion on its fitness. His opinion was read to the assembled company and recorded in the minute book. The opening lines of his verdict were damning:

> Having surveyed the Corn Exchange and Stores recently erected in East Street I have to report that I find the timber in many respects much to [*sic*] weak and injudiciously constructed – the roof of the exchange cannot be deemed safe and in my opinion it is necessary to take it off and put on a new one constructed on a better principle. In the stores the Common Joists are much too slight for their bearing.

The committee resolved to replace the roof and the first floor, and requested that Savage prepare plans and estimates for the works he had identified. At the annual general meeting on 4 May 1836 the committee reported that £441 15s. 11d. had been expended on repairs, and it was resolved to commence proceedings against Draper as recommended by counsel.

Again, without the all-important committee minute book we know not whether the actions against Draper were successful, and it is odd that none of this excitement was reported in the press. At the time the *Hampshire*

Telegraph correspondent was busy reporting on the proceedings of both the Literary and Philosophical Society and the Mechanics' Institute, and the new premises being built in Southgate for the latter; he had obviously lost interest in the Corn Exchange. The repair works must have been highly disruptive to business, but trading seems to have carried on regardless.

After this more works were proposed to the Corn Exchange, a notice for which was placed in the *Hampshire Telegraph* dated 23 August 1836, inviting builders to tender for 'certain ALTERATIONS to be made to the Corn Exchange in the City of Chichester' and stating that plans and specifications could be inspected at the office of Mr John Elliott of South Street, Chichester. Elliott has now appeared on the scene.

John Elliott, who was both an architect and a builder, designed Chichester's Mechanics' Institute in Southgate in 1835,[135] and had completed the east wing of Goodwood House between 1838 and 1839.[136] In November 1837 he wrote to the corporation seeking appointment as city surveyor, but failed to secure the post – the corporation's tactful response being that 'no order had been made thereon'.[137]

In connection with these alterations, in September 1836 Mr Dendy, the chairman, applied to the Paving Commissioners for permission to remove the columns from the front of the exchange and to re-erect them on the pavement 'at about six feet from their present position', to which the commissioners agreed.[138] The following month, on 4 October, they revised their application, intending now to move the columns to the extremity of the pavement 'to the plan produced by Mr Elliott', and permission was

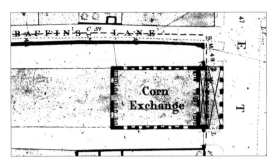

46 *An extract from the 1875 1:500 scale Ordnance Survey that shows the internal layout of the trading hall. The new inner wall behind the columns added by Elliott can be seen as can the traders' stands at each end of the hall. The internal layout of the corn stores to the south is not indicated. The thick line to the west of the Corn Exchange represents the wall that separated the site from Baffins Lane.*

also duly granted. Unusually the corporation did not make the company take out a lease for the area of pavement upon which the columns stood.

Thus it was Elliott who was brought in to remodel the trading hall into the form we now know. Elliott reduced the number of columns on the original frontage from six to four and had four more cast to make up the new row of six at the pavement edge.

The solution to the Draper/Elliott conundrum is now clear. Draper was rebuffed by the legal proceedings brought against him and, doubtless more than slighted by the fact that Elliott had remodelled the building, he no longer felt the Corn Exchange to be his own work. When he wrote the entry on the Corn Exchange for the *Dictionary of Architecture* he washed his hands of it and attributed it to Elliott instead!

Frustratingly the rebuilding work and the erection of the new columns, which should have been quite exciting, failed to excite the *Hampshire Telegraph* correspondent, who refrained from making any reports about the work.

Elliott had extended the roofline forward so that it covered the pavement to create a narthex supported on an impressive pedimented portico of six cast-iron columns, the four new ones matching the originals exactly. From the photograph given in Fig. 46 it can be seen that Elliott retained Draper's side gates, but the pavilions were demolished and the gates reset on simple piers set further back. There are still iron gates between the inner columns, but beyond them a solid wall has been constructed to close off the trading hall from the street. The remodelled building was much more convenient, especially in winter.

The remodelled Corn Exchange was now an impressive Greek-revival temple, and its detailing was much stronger than Elliott's own Mechanics' Institute built in the same style the previous year. Its forward building line would catch the eye of anyone looking along East Street, giving the Corn Exchange an enviably commanding presence in the city's prime commercial street. The only detraction would have been that beast market, held right in front of it once a fortnight.

Six

The Corn Market 1833-1947

With the opening of the Corn Exchange the business of the corn market seems to have transferred thither, lock, stock and barrel. The records of the Chichester Corn Exchange Co. provide a fascinating insight into the volatility of the corn trade and its effects upon the company's fortunes. The following figures for receipt of corn were recorded in the shareholders' minute book[139] for the period 1 May 1833 to 30 April 1834, the first full year of trading:

Quantities of corn received into the stores:

	Quarters	Bushels
Wheat	9,860	3½
Barley	3,256	4
Oats	1,045	0
Beans	176	0
Peas	229	2
Tares	142	2
Seeds	98	3
Total	14,807	6½

The receipts amounted to £206 0s. 11d. with a further £43 14s. 4d. owing, giving a total income of £329 15s. 3d. The above statistics also tell us the various types of crop being handled, which were more than those one might expect to go under the generic term corn. The most surprising of these perhaps is tares, a term one might first associate with its biblical meaning of a weed that is actually a menace in the cornfield. In the parable of the wheat and the tares an enemy sows weed seeds (tares) among the newly sown wheat in an act of sabotage, and the farmer orders that the two be allowed to grow together until harvest when the tares will be gathered and burnt.[140] Tare was also a term used for a variant of the vetch (*vicia*) family, while an 18th-century dictionary definition is 'a weed that grows among corn'.

47 *A Victorian engraving of the Corn Exchange, in the form recognisable today. Note the chains at the edge of the roadway intended to prevent cattle from the adjacent beast market straying onto the pavement.*

The Rev. Arthur Young, in his *General View of the Agriculture of the County of Sussex* of 1808, provides the answer to the puzzle, namely that tares (meaning vetch) were grown as animal feed, the seeds being sown among the stubble after harvest and animals being let into the field in the spring to consume the results. Young reckoned an acre of tares at 4d. per week for ewes and lambs to be worth 40 to 60s., and opined that tares 'are of such infinite importance that not one half of the stock could be maintained without them'. Tares were thus a valuable cash crop, hence the provision for the trade in their seed at the Corn Exchange.

Throughput of corn and dividends paid 1833-63

Year	Corn received q-bsh	Total Dividend £ s. d.			Remarks
1833-4	14,807-6½	0			
1834-5	14,298-5	0			
1835-6	16,585-4	37	10	0	first dividend paid
1837-8	18,342 -0	10	0	0	
1842-3	24,768-3	24	0	0	
1847-8	39,558-7	117	0	0	
1850-1	45,662-5	125	0	0	
1857-8	52,859-0	482	0	0	peak throughput
1860-1	48,157-7½	600	0	0	
1862-3	43,570-2½	600	0	0	

It can be seen that once the building problems were ironed out in 1835-6 shareholder dividends began to be paid, and the throughput increased steadily to peak at 52,859 quarters in 1862-3, after which it dropped to a plateau averaging around 46,500 quarters. This plateau continued until 1871.

On 13 June 1838 Henry Sadler, who had subscribed to £100-worth of shares, was elected to the committee of the company, remaining so until his death in 1877,[141] and this began a long association of his family with the Corn Exchange. Each year the minutes of the annual general meetings reflect that all was going well and several resolutions were taken to improve the efficiency of the operation. In 1847 insurance cover was increased to £12,000, and the following year it was resolved that the Corn Exchange would not be open for business on Good Friday and 'days of humbler fasts'. The company resolved to ban smoking in their premises in 1855, with any person persisting in so doing being 'forthwith removed from the building and premises'. As it took the rest of England until 2007 to ban smoking in public places, the Chichester Corn Exchange Company was very forward-looking in this respect – but unfortunately they were not to be so in most others.

The year 1858, in addition to being when its business reached a peak, saw some changes in the way the Corn Exchange operated. In December it was resolved to erect stands at the south and north ends of the trading

48 *A view of the interior of the Corn Exchange trading hall in the 1860s, looking south towards the corn store. The portrait over the door is of Charles Gordon Lennox (later 5th Duke of Richmond), who became the first president of the Royal Agricultural Society in 1840. In the blocked window to the left the rules of the Corn Exchange are displayed and around the walls can be seen the traders' stands. In the centre sacks of corn have been pitched against the rails. The trading hall is lit by pairs of gasoliers.*

RULES
OF THE
CHICHESTER
CORN EXCHANGE.

The Exchange to be Open for the Receipt and De-
livery of Corn every day (except Sunday, Christmas
Day and Good Friday) from 6 a.m. to 5 p.m.
The Exchange to be Open for the Sale of Corn
every Wednesday from 12 till 2 o'Clock.
No Corn or Grain to be sold except on Market Days.
Sample Sacks to be arranged alphabetically.
No sample Sacks to be shewn unless the bulk be
deposited in the Stores.

THE FOLLOWING

Tolls to be Paid to the Clerk :

	s.	*d.*
For every Load of 5 qrs. of Corn or Grain, received into the Stores	1	0
Ditto, delivered from the Stores	0	6
For every Sack of Clover or other Seed received into the Stores	0	6
No Quantity of Corn or Seed (except the immediate Residue of a larger Quantity) will be delivered from the Stores, at a less Charge than	0	6

A Penny for every Load of Corn or Grain, or any quantity less than a Load, to be paid
for Insurance from Fire.
An additional Charge of Sixpence per Load per week, to be made for every Load of Corn
and Grain remaining in the Stores more than six weeks.
A Commission of One Shilling per Load for Selling, and Two Shillings per Load for
Buying, to be paid to the Clerk.
No Corn will be delivered except on the production of a Ticket or Written Order, signed
by the Seller, stating to whom the Sale is made; and, if to more than one person, the Quantity
to each.
☞ The Committee are not to be considered responsible for the payment of the value of
any Corn or Grain sold by the Clerk on commission.
It is requested that all empty Sacks returned to the Stores should be labelled with the
number of Sacks, and the name of the Party from whom they are sent.

R. RAPER,
SECRETARY.

Mason, Printer.

49 *A printed copy of the rules of the Corn Exchange. It is undated but carries a watermark of 1850.*

hall (one must assume that before this date they were only along the sides) and that the rent of each stand should be £5 annually, paid in advance. These new stands can be seen in the fine interior view given as Fig. 49. Henry Sadler then proposed that those living some distance from the Corn Exchange be afforded the privilege of selling their corn by sample 'on payment of one guinea a year'. This represented a major change in policy but certainly a welcome one.[142]

Another momentous decision that year was that to provide an additional urinal, 'the present accommodation be-ing very deficient in that respect'. One can quite understand the deficiency: consumption of much beer on market days was an occupational hazard in the farming line. That same year James Hack, the founder, died, and his holding of 10 shares was auctioned as part of his estate on 26 June. All realised their £25 face value, reflecting continuing confidence in the corn trade and the company's role in it.[143]

The rules of the Corn Exchange, i.e. the conditions upon which trade was carried out, were revised once in January 1859 and again in May. The principal changes related to charges, which became:

[1]   Merchants or Dealers using stands – £5 per annum.
[2]   Ditto not using stands – £2 per annum.
[3]   Farmers to be allowed to sell their own corn by sample at £1 per annum but if charge for storage for the year amounts to 40/- then the £1 should be returned. No sample bags allowed in the settling room.
[4]   Charges to be paid in advance to the Clerk.
[5]   Applications for desks to be made to the Clerk.
[6]   Rules to be applicable from 25 March last [i.e. 25 March 1859].

The New Corn Store

So briskly did the business expand that by 1843 the corn store in Baffin's Lane was proving too small to hold all the incoming produce, as

50 *An extract from the 1896 1:2500-scale Ordnance Survey showing the Corn Exchange 'campus' completed. The New Corn Store stands to the east of the original building and the position of the footbridge linking the buildings at first-floor level is indicated.*

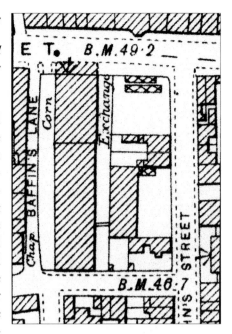

was noted at a special shareholders' meeting held on 30 August that year:[144] 'That in consequence of the increased and increasing quantity of Corn being brought into the Corn Exchange it is incumbent on the Proprietors to take into consideration the best means of enlarging the stores to meet the wants of the Agriculturalists and the interests of the Shareholders.' No action was taken until May 1862, when it was announced to the annual general meeting that Mr G.T. Dendy (who at the time was company chairman) had purchased four lots of building land adjoining the Corn Exchange for the sum of £340 and offered it to the shareholders for the same amount to build a new corn store. His offer was accepted.

The land concerned was on the west side of St John's Street, a part of Crosbie's New Town that had remained undeveloped and which in 1862 had just been conveyed to Benjamin Binstead.[145] Despite Dendy's magnanimous gesture nothing was to happen on the site for a further nine years, and the accounts show that in the meantime it was being rented out for use as a garden. Finally, at the annual general meeting of 17 May 1871, it was announced that the tender from Mr Gammon had been accepted to build the New Corn Store for £880, and that the additional monies needed to fund the project would be borrowed from the bankers.

51 *The now badly eroded foundation stone to the New Corn Store.*

The foundation stone, which is visible on the west side of the building, was laid by the chairman on 17 June 1871, as its inscription records:

Laid by G T Dendy Esq
Chairman of CCEC
June 17th 1871
Geo Elkington – Arch

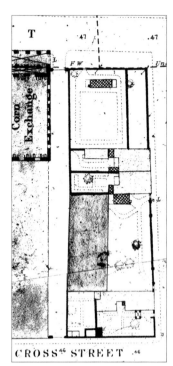

52 *An extract from the 1875 1:500-scale Ordnance Survey map showing, centre and shaded, the New Corn Store. To the east of it is a garden, complete with greenhouse, which is separated from St John's Street by a wall. Cross Street was later renamed New Town.*

About the architect, Mr Elkington, little is known, but the building he provided is not unattractive and is worthy of its New Town setting. It is of two storeys and built of flint with red-brick dressings, under a slate roof. The first floor was supported on 14 cast-iron columns, which were made that July by Halsted and Sons at their foundry just around the corner in East Pallant.[146]

As built, the New Corn Store faced onto the eastern access road and was linked in 1893 to the old corn stores at first-floor level by the now-vanished footbridge indicated on the Ordnance Survey map in Fig. 51. The elevation facing St John's Street was thus the rear of the building, and the unused land to its east was left as a garden, screened from the street by a wall. The letting-out of this garden provided an additional source of income for the company.[147]

With the benefit of hindsight, the investment in a new corn store can be seen as rather unwise, since in 1871 (the year of its construction) the intake of corn began to plummet, and another agricultural depression was fast approaching, one that would quickly render the building surplus to requirements. At the committee meeting of 15 October 1884 it was agreed to let the upper floor to Mr Caffin for use as a corn store for six months at a rate of £50. Mr Caffin was a member of the committee, so his wishing to hire part of the redundant corn store for its intended purpose is questionable

53 *The New Corn Store viewed from St John's Street, 2003. This was originally the rear of the building. The fenestration has been much altered since it ceased to be used for its original purpose and was re-orientated to front onto St John's Street. It is now used as offices.*

to say the least. It would appear that he was setting up in competition to the Corn Exchange Company, but no one seemed to comment on it.[148]

The declining corn trade

Throughput of corn and dividends paid 1869-1900

Year	Corn received, q. bsh.		Total Dividend paid out	Remarks
1869-70	41,620	5	£720	
1870-1	43,340	6½	£720	
1871-2	35,963	7	£720	New Corn Store opens
1878-9	31,740	6½	£660	Agricultural depression starts
1883-4	26,994	4	£680	New Corn Store partly redundant
1887-8	19,429	1½	£480	
1890-1	16,085	2	£540	Wool trading starts
1893-4	10,041	7	£600	
1897-8	10,422	7	£300	
1899-1900	8,993	0	£300	New Corn Store almost redundant

From Table 2 above, which as before gives just two indicators of the company's health for selected years, it can be seen that business in the corn trade was falling off rapidly and that the shareholder dividend suffered as a result. All through this period there were problems with customers who defaulted on their payments for goods and services received, and several had to be threatened with court action.

The unhappy state of trading was not lamented, or even obliquely referred to, at the annual general meetings, which is strange since the attending shareholders were being hit in the pocket. There was, however, evidence of much belt-tightening, such as at the meeting of 7 May 1879 when a memorandum presented by traders requesting the installation of wooden flooring in place of the flagstones 'to add to the comfort and beneficially affect the health of those trading' was met with outright refusal, the poor traders being left to suffer the effects of the cold and damp in stoic silence.

To compensate for the decline in corn trading, the company added two new commodities to their trade in 1890, namely hops and wool, and Wyatt's the auctioneers then carried out regular wool sales in the trading hall. Additional income was obtained by allowing Halsted and Sons to display their agricultural implements on the access roads, doubtless in the hope that farmers who had done particularly well in trading at the beast market might be tempted to invest in a new plough or horse hoe. Halsted's, who were also perhaps feeling the pinch, made several applications to have the 2s. 6d. daily charge for this reduced, but no such concessions were ever granted.[149] A similar source of additional income

54 *The plaque put up in 1996 to commemorate the centenary of the first public showing of films in Chichester, which took place at the Corn Exchange.*

came from allowing advertising hoardings to be attached to the sides of the buildings, and some of these are apparent in early photographs of the Corn Exchange.

Further new business directions saw an increase in the hiring of the trading hall for entertainment purposes, and the Corn Exchange made a significant contribution to Chichester's history on Boxing Day 1896 when, as part of her annual pantomime, Maggie Morton staged the first film showing in the city. The films shown were all short, but included one entitled 'Gardeners burning weeds'. While this title might not itself be expected to guarantee a queue all the way down Baffins Lane, it would still have caused much excitement among the public. This historic event was commemorated by a plaque affixed to the Corn Exchange in 1996 which, sadly, goes unnoticed by most Cicestrians.

New century

The new century did not usher in much in the way of new hope for the Chichester Corn Exchange Company, as business in corn trading continued to plummet to a staggering low; the following table indicates a drop of 74 per cent in throughput over the space of five years, although the dividends had begun to rise again after 1903:

Throughput of corn and dividends paid 1901-5

Year	Corn received, q.-bsh.	Total Dividend paid out, £
1900-1	6,887-4	420
1901-2	4,184-4	360
1902-3	4,642-4	300
1903-4	4,054-0	330
1904-5	1,801-4	410

As a result of the company entering the wool market, the woolstapling firm of Prior's, whose premises were in Tower Street, hired the now unused top floor of the old corn store as extra storage space. There was still need for restraint, however, and at their meeting of 18 July 1900 the committee decided once again to defer the long-overdue repainting of the outside of the Corn Exchange. The following year the National Telephone Company were allowed to install an instrument 'for the convenience of the standholders', but this had to be at no cost to the company.[150]

Expansion of the alternative uses for the trading hall, other than on market days of course, brought theatrical performances, roller skating and film shows, and in 1903 a proper stage was installed. This side of the company's business is a fascinating story in itself and could fill several chapters, but for the purposes of Chichester's market story we must concentrate on corn trading.

The limited company

Back in December 1901, following the death of Sir Robert George Raper, the post of company secretary was filled by W.B.B. Freeland. William Bennett Barton Freeland (to give him his full name) had been born in Steyning in 1845, and was nephew by marriage of Robert George Raper; like him he also became a solicitor with Johnson & Co.[151]

On his appointment Freeland immediately floated the idea of turning the organisation into a limited company, understanding as he did the

55   *A view of the Corn Exchange, c.1905. Propped against the nearest column is a board proclaiming 'SALE NOW ON', while to the left the theatre billboard advertises a production by the Charley's Aunt Company. The horse and cart to the left belonged to Fred Sadler, who was later to become very involved with the Corn Exchange.*

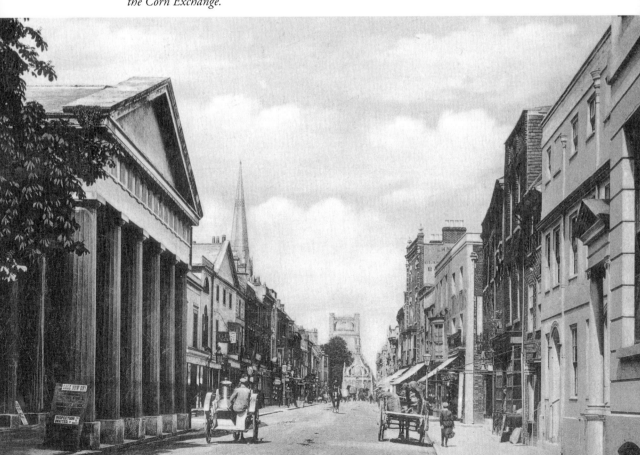

56 *A souvenir porcelain cup and saucer of German manufacture titled 'A Present from Chichester'. Such wares were very popular in the late 19th and early 20th centuries, and here the Corn Exchange was deemed worthy of being included on both the cup and the saucer, doubtless owing to the building's importance as a centre of entertainment.*

advantages to be gained from limiting the company's liability. He received absolutely no support for this but the matter resurfaced in 1905, and at an extraordinary general meeting convened to debate the issue on 8 March the following proposal was laid before the shareholders:[152]

> That for defining and re-tendering the Object for which the Exchange was formed and to enable the Committee to legally utilize the Exchange buildings for any purpose for which it is now used, or for any other purpose which the Committee may think desirable, the Rules now laid on the table and read to the Shareholders which have been open to their inspection during the last seven days [should be adopted].

The solecism of the split infinitive – an early instance thereof – may be excused by the pressure under which the committee found themselves. The motion to incorporate the company, with its liability limited by shares under section 179 of the Companies Act 1862, was carried, and it would henceforward be known as Chichester Corn Exchange Limited.

The new set of rules had been drawn up by the legal firm of Raper, Freeland and Tyacke,* and in its 41 sections, as well as setting out the responsibilities of the new directors, it redefined the objects of the company, giving wide-reaching powers to attract new business in the fields of entertainment to compensate for the collapsing corn market.

Another extraordinary general meeting was held on 23 August 1905 to elect directors to the new limited company in accordance with the Companies Act. The appointments were Messrs A.E. Woodbridge as

---

* This practice had grown out of Johnson and Co., of which W.B.B. Freeland was part, with Raper now appearing in the company name. It still had its office at 55 West Street.

chairman and W.B.B. Freeland as secretary, along with Messrs A. Purchase, E. Critchell, C.C. Combes, H. Sadler, F. Hardham, W.P. Cogan and E.W. Humphry as ordinary directors. A new directors' minute book was started, and with it a new style of recording.[153] The annual general meetings were now written up in a separate shareholders' minute book, and printed papers giving the chairman's report, trading figures and the all-important share dividends were distributed to the shareholders, but few of these have survived.[154] Also discontinued were the useful compilations of throughput of commodities, which is a pity as the continuing downward trend in the corn trade cannot be followed; perhaps it was becoming so pitiful that the committee deemed it unworthy of being recorded.

The change of company status necessitated a reissue of the share certificates, and the momentous decision was taken to redesign them, replacing at long last the old image of the Corn Exchange (which it had ceased to resemble 69 years previously) with one reflecting its current appearance.[155]

By 1905 the New Corn Store had become completely surplus to requirements, the original corn store in Baffins Lane having more than enough capacity for the reduced corn trade. From this point it was leased out for other purposes, and the only part it played in the Corn Exchange Company's business was in providing income in the form of rent.*

The company continued with the weekly corn market on Wednesdays, and the half-yearly dividend remained at a constant 15s. per share.[156]

When Mr F. Hardham, one of the original directors, resigned in October 1910, his place was taken by Oliver N. Wyatt, a member of the long-established Chichester firm of estate agents and auctioneers, beginning a long family association with the company. He was promoted to chairman four years later when A.E. Woodbridge, who had been chairman for 20 years, died.

57 *The new design of share certificate reflecting the change in the company's status. This certificate is in the name of Frederick Sadler, who was to become a major shareholder over the course of the following 30 years.*

---

* For the subsequent story of this building, see the author's *St John's Chapel and the New Town, Chichester*, Phillimore, 2005.

58 *The bronze plaque below the stained-glass window in St Paul's Church at Northgate, given as a memorial to the 9th Cyclist Battalion of the Hampshire Regiment who spent part of the First World War billeted at the Corn Exchange.*

The First World War

War broke out on 4 August 1914, and the Corn Exchange was called up to play its part when the building was used to billet the 242 troops of the 2nd/9th Cyclist Battalion of the Hampshire Regiment. This should have provided a useful additional income stream, but unfortunately the army proved to be reluctant payers and the company had to conduct their own battles to get their rent. The occupation was short lived, as the Hampshire Regiment moved out in May 1915. They left their mark on the city by donating, in 1919, a stained-glass memorial window to St Paul's Church at Northgate, a gift commemorated in a bronze plaque that can still be seen in the south-east corner of the church.

The survival of a few printed reports for the period around the First World War enables an analysis to be carried out of the company's trading during that time, including a split of income between the intended corn trade and the hire of the trading hall for entertainments. After a one-off zero dividend of 1914, the by now standard 15s. per share was paid out until the end of 1917, after which it dropped to 8s. in June 1918, rising to 10s. the following November.[157]

Analysis of income 1907-19

Year	Income from corn			Income from hire			% of total
	£	s.	d.	£	s.	d.	as hire
1907	£440	0	3	208	12	9	32
1908	£471	17	11	231	13	9	32
1911	£467	3	6	293	2	11	38
1912	£522	14	9	306	10	5	36
1913	£419	15	7	381	17	0	48
1914	£425	4	4	316	9	9	43
1915	£421	7	9	315	15	0	43
1919	£466	2	9	215	15	0	32

In the above, corn comprises income from rent of stands, subscriptions, selling, storage and receipt and delivery of sacks; hire comprises hire of hall, and repayments made by hirers in respect of gas and the performance licence. From this it can be seen that, despite having shrunk drastically since the mid-19th century, trading in corn was still the core business of the company.

Comments made by the chairman in the annual reports about the health of the company are interesting. In 1913 he states that 'the finances of the Company are in excellent condition, notwithstanding the fact that the receipts for storage shew a considerable diminution', while in 1915 he points out that the profits had actually been increased by the military occupation of the buildings. In 1917, as the effects of the war made international trade more difficult, the government demanded that more land be made over to the growing of crops rather than being put to grass, and this may be why the corn income had risen by 1919. This revival was brief, however, as after the war much agricultural land in Sussex returned to grassland again.[158]

The year 1925 was particularly tight for the company and a review of the market charges was carried out. They decided that these needed to be increased, and wrote to the local branch of the National Farmers' Union (NFU) to seek a meeting to discuss the same.

In the middle of all this O.N. Wyatt decided to resign from the board of directors and the chairman, T.S. Adcock, died in office. Adcock was quickly replaced by G.S. Pitts, who was catapulted into the brewing storm with the NFU. The meeting with the NFU had obviously not gone as well as the directors had hoped, for at their meeting of 18 November a letter from the NFU was read out dictating the terms under which the NFU was prepared to operate at the Corn Exchange:

> The NFU Branch to pay one annual subscription of £1.
> The Corn Exchange Company to guarantee no charge for admission to NFU members for the next 25 years.
> NFU Members to be issued with admission tickets, for each of which the Company would be paid 1s.
> One Company director to be appointed by the NFU – the NFU buying at least one share to entitle them to such a position.

To this the board partly acquiesced, resolving that 'all bona fide farmers, who have no other business but that of farming, whether members of the National Farmers' Union or not, have free access to the Corn Exchange on the recognised market days. All other persons without exception to be charged the usual annual subscription.' In other words farmers would get in free but dealers would not.[159]

A strong wind of change

Back in 1921 the Corn Exchange Company, instead of managing the individual hirings of the trading hall themselves, began to grant leases to theatrical companies, who could have sole use of it or sublet to others as they wished, except on Wednesdays when the corn market was held. This was

59 *A view of the Baffins Lane corn store when it had also become the Corn Exchange, as denoted by the sign over the door.*

taken a step further in 1927 when, after a long period on negotiation with the then current tenant, the Corn Exchange Company agreed to a 35-year exclusive full-repairing lease of the trading hall so as to allow it to be converted into a bespoke theatre. Work was carried out in the autumn of 1927 to install raked seating and a proscenium-arch stage, creating the Exchange Theatre, which opened its doors on 29 November.[160]

This, of course, required the company to surrender its use of the trading hall for the weekly corn market, and under the terms of his lease the lessee had to carry out work at his own expense to convert part of the Baffins Lane corn store into a new corn exchange. It should be pointed out that the Exchange Theatre also took over the first (northern) five bays of the Baffins Lane building – a further reflection of how the corn trade had shrunk, freeing up space for storage.[161]

Thus, following commencement of the works to convert the trading hall into a theatre, the entire business of the Corn Exchange retreated 'backstage' into the corn store. The modifications carried out there to provide a new trading hall included opening up the blind arched windows to improve the light, the laying of a 'jointless floor',* repairs to the roof and a new ladies' lavatory. The Corn Exchange Company invested £48 in overhauling the market stands.

Curiously no notices were placed in the local press about the re-siting of the weekly corn market; instead the general public was made aware of the new arrangements by way of the installation of two new Corn

60 *The nameplate from D. Combes's stand in the 'new' Corn Exchange. Dudley Combes was one of three major seed merchants in the city at the time.*

---

* This was probably the patent timber block flooring system manufactured in Germany by Junkers.

Exchange signs, one over the porch in Baffins Lane and the other at the rear entrance in the private roadway.[162] One can only suppose that, as the regular traders would have been advised in person at the last market to be held in the main hall, any such notice was deemed unnecessary. In 1927 there were 45 paid-up stand-holders listed in the company's cash book, but it is unlikely that all would have been operative at every sale.[163]

The reduced scale of the corn trade meant that the loss of storage space caused by moving the corn market onto the ground floor of the stores caused the company no great hardship. Indeed, in May 1929 they placed an advertisement in the *West Sussex Gazette* for letting out spare storage space.

Although the theatre was now outside their control, the Corn Exchange Company remained in the entertainment business by hiring out the new Corn Exchange, particularly for dancing, which was the reason for the jointless floor being installed.

Financial problems

The year of 1929 marked the start of yet another round of financial difficulties, with overdrafts having to be arranged with the bankers. In May the rate demand for the premises risked crippling the finances, so it was resolved to submit an appeal against it; but this was soon abandoned when legal advice declared the prospects of winning to be rather poor.

More overdrafts followed in 1930 and 1931 in order to keep the company afloat, and in 1933 heavy expenditure on the fabric provided a major drain in resources, bringing about the need for yet another overdraft of £200 and a decision to sell some war stock to raise a further £203.[164]

Between 1927 and 1930 dividends paid to the shareholders had held up, with the payments typically being £1 per share in May and 15s. in November, but at a special meeting in June it was resolved that no dividend would be declared at the AGM owing to the 'unfavourable position of the company from a financial point of view and the recent heavy assessment for Income Tax'. A dividend of 10s. was able to be paid the following November, however.[165]

On the subject of shareholders, it is instructional to examine the names of those who had the largest individual holdings of the 240 shares. Thomas Adcock, who became a director in 1911 and was elected chairman in 1921, held 40 shares in 1915, increasing to 46 in 1926, while Conrade Combes, another director and father of the founder of the Chichester firm of seed merchants, held 10 in 1915, rising to 19 in 1933. The most significant increase in holdings, though, was that of another corn and seed merchant, Frederick Sadler. He owned eight shares in 1915, 37 in 1924, and his holding then increased steadily to reach 58 by 1935.[166] In 1929 Sadler had rented a floor of the corn exchange for six months for his own corn business, which provided a hint of the way things were to go in the 1950s. The importance of these two corn merchants in the story of the corn market will be covered fully in Chapter Eight.

Baffins Lane

Baffins Lane, which ran along the western side of the Corn Exchange site, was originally very narrow and the new buildings had been set back from it in order to create a private access road, separated from the public highway by a brick wall. In 1925 the idea was floated of demolishing the wall and selling the private road to the corporation in order to widen Baffins Lane, but the idea was quickly squashed. However, when in February 1928 part of the wall fell down it was resolved to demolish the remains and replace it with iron railings.

Frederick Sadler made a bid at an extraordinary general meeting of the shareholders, held on 6 August 1935, to take on a lease of the access road to create a commercial car park. This was agreed to, and he was granted the right to remove the iron railings on condition that, as well as maintaining the roadway, he marked the company's boundary with stones and cast-iron sockets into which could be placed loose posts and chains. Once a year the posts and chains had to be erected in order to prevent the private roadway from becoming a public right of way. The other condition was that that he granted free parking to Corn Exchange officials and stand-holders.[167] The fixed fence was removed, and each Christmas Day the temporary stopping up was duly carried out.[168]

The corporation was still very keen to acquire the private road and approached the company again in 1936, but without success. It was not until 1948, following the demise of the company, that the transfer finally took place, and Baffins Lane was widened with a new pavement abutting the west wall of the Corn Exchange – the arrangement that exists today.[169]

61 *A view along Baffins Lane on a gloomy day in the late 1930s. To the right can be seen the narrow carriageway of Baffins Lane itself, flanked by its flagged pavement, while the wider area to the left is the Corn Exchange Company's private road. By this time the wall that previously separated the two had been demolished, and the line of sockets to take the temporary posts and chains, installed each Christmas Day to prevent the road becoming a right of way, can be seen at the back of the pavement line.*

The demise of the Corn Exchange Company

Unfortunately the last directors' minute book, covering the years 1933 to 1948, and the accompanying dividend and cash books beyond 1941 are missing, so the story of the run-up to the company's demise has to be deduced from the shareholders' minute book (which only records the AGMs) and various other sources.

Annual reports for the war years 1942 to 1945 indicate that corn trading continued, albeit with declining receipts, but the rental of the cinema provided a steady income, keeping the business in profit and allowing good dividends to be declared, that in 1943 being 4½ per cent – £1 2s. 6d. per share.[170]

The year 1946 was an important one for the future of the Chichester Corn Exchange Company and, as a result, corn trading in Chichester. At the annual general meeting in June an increase in income from the market was reported and a record dividend of 7½ per cent (£1 17s. 6d. per share) was declared, but no hint was given of the storm gathering on the horizon. On 18 November a special general meeting of shareholders was called, attended by 18 thereof,* who all signed the minute book to record their presence, and T.G. Purchase, seconded by Dudley Combes, proposed that an offer to purchase the freehold of the company's premises be accepted, noting that the company was liable for the repairs to the cinema roof. This last referred to the aftermath of a fire that had occurred just three days before.[171]

The name of the prospective purchaser is not quoted in the shareholders' minutes so we have to turn to the *Chichester Observer* for this vital piece of information. In a front-page article in their edition of 21 December 1946 they reported that the Corn Exchange and the Exchange Cinema were being bought by a Mr George Booth, who was proposing to develop the site as an arts centre.

At an extraordinary general meeting held on 12 March 1947 it was reported that the freehold had been sold, the money deposited at the bank, and that the chairman, George Pitts, had 'stated circumstances in which a winding-up had become desirable'. The special resolution for the voluntary winding-up was proposed by Pitts, seconded by Frederick Sadler senior, and carried unanimously by the assembled shareholders. The company's fate had been sealed, and with that the minutes unceremoniously come to an abrupt end; the rest of the book's pages are blank.[172]

The necessary public notice was placed in the 22 April 1947 issue of the *London Gazette*, stating that Chichester Corn Exchange Ltd was

---

* The 18 shareholders represented 204 of the 240 holdings, so a majority view was expressed.

going into voluntary liquidation and creditors were invited to send details of their claims to Raper and Co., who were acting as solicitors for Jack Thompson, the liquidator. The *Chichester Observer*, although carrying the same legal notice, made no report about the impending demise of one of the city's longest-running businesses, so we do not know the date of the last day's trading.

The freehold had been sold for £28,468 4s. 0d., which, after paying legal charges and commissions, netted £21,524 7s. 3d. for the coffers.[173] The process of liquidation dragged on with the inevitable legal prolongation until finally, in its issue of 21 September 1948, the *London Gazette* carried a notice to the effect that the winding-up of the company was complete and that the liquidator's account would be presented to shareholders at a meeting to be held at Raper's offices at 55 West Street on Wednesday 27 October 1948.

The final (undated) liquidator's report shewed the total value of the company's assets to be £29,173 10s. 5d., out of which £942 5s. 8d. was owed to creditors. After paying the expenses of the liquidation, the shareholders received an interim return of £100 per £25 share on 21 May 1947 and a final return of £14 10s. on 6 October 1948. It will be noticed that the share certificate illustrated in Fig. 58 has been endorsed with the dates these payments were made. The liquidator's remuneration was £525 – a modest 1.79 per cent of the value of the company, but the entries in the *London Gazette* had cost an incredible £15 each.[174]

With the collapse of the Corn Exchange Company, Chichester was now without a corn market, but the corporation took an unexpected interest in its plight and proposed to re-site it at the Cattle Market. The city surveyor drew up plans for a building containing 56 stands with a frontage onto Market Road and this was approved by the Markets Committee on 19 July 1950. Construction was deferred the following October and then the idea was quickly abandoned.[175] However, the Corn Exchange was to be revived in 1951, as we shall see in Chapter Seven.

In 1950 the moribund Corn Exchange buildings were added to the statutory list, which ensured their survival. The former trading hall, now the cinema, was Grade II* and the rear portion in Baffins Lane Grade II.

George Booth abandoned his scheme for an arts centre in 1951 and sold on the Baffins Lane and cinema buildings, retaining only the New Corn Store. This became a dancing school bearing his name, the Booth Rooms.

SEVEN

Sadler's, Combes and the Revival of the Corn Market, 1951-75

After George Booth abandoned his project to convert the Corn Exchange into an arts centre, he sold the freehold of the buildings, the cinema to Granada and the Baffins Lane building to Sadler and Co.[176] As Booth had hinted in an article in the *Chichester Observer*, the Corn Exchange (or rather a part of it) was about to be returned to its original purpose.

The two subsequent reincarnations of the corn market came about by the intervention of two of Chichester's major corn merchants, Sadler & Co. between 1951 and 1966 and D. Combes from 1966 to 1975. The Sadler and Combes families had been associated with the Corn Exchange Company from its beginning in 1832, and so are worthy of a little study.

Sadler's of Chichester

The Sadlers are an ancient Sussex family whose origins can be traced back some 500 years; there are many family headstones to be seen at Bepton church.[177] Henry Sadler, a yeoman of Langford, Mid Lavant, was one of the original investors in the Corn Exchange Company and was elected onto the committee in 1834, serving until 1872 when his attendances cease. On his death in 1877 his extensive estate was sold by auction by Wyatt and Co. of Chichester, and it included a dwelling house, woolstore and stable in Little London as well as five shares in the Corn Exchange Company.[178] Another Henry Sadler, probably the first Henry Sadler's son, first attended an AGM in 1883 and was elected onto the committee in 1888. He became one of the first directors when the limited company was set up in 1905, serving as such until his death in 1916.[179]

The entry of Sadler's into the corn and seed business was not down to either of these gentlemen but to Robert Sadler, who in 1886 acquired the corn and seed merchant business of John E. Toogood at 40 East Street,

62 *Sadler's Shop at 40 East Street, c.1897. At this time it was being run by Fred Sadler, who had taken over the business from Robert in 1895.*

63 *Fred Sadler, who ran the family business from 1895 to 1961, standing in the garden of his Little London house with his dog Bonzo.*

conveniently sited opposite the Corn Exchange.[180] When O.N. Wyatt carried out a valuation of Toogood's business on Robert Sadler's behalf, he reckoned the stock in trade to be worth £25 1s. 3d. and the fixtures and fittings £36 6s. 0d. The stock in trade included seeds, meal, dog biscuits, sacks, straw and hay plus the fittings, a push cart on springs, measures, seed cases and a chaff cutter.[181]

Also involved in the business was his son Frederick (Fred), who was to expand Sadler's into the largest corn merchant's business in Chichester. Fred was a born entrepreneur but also a tough man to work for, expecting a very full day's work from his staff. When Robert died in 1895 Fred took over, changing the name to Sadler & Co. in 1897 and to F. Sadler & Co. in 1900.[182]

Fred had invested in Corn Exchange shares, becoming one of its first directors when the limited company was set up in 1905, and steadily increasing his shareholding to 58 by 1935. Naturally he also rented a stand in the Corn Exchange for his own trading.

The business of Sadler's grew rapidly under Fred's direction, and in 1905 he acquired an 18th-century store in Little London as his main storage facility, a building round the corner in East Row to house a seed-processing plant, and another building opposite that was used as a sack store. These buildings he bought from Messrs W. & J. Smith for £1,750.[183] Westhampnett Mill was then acquired and converted into an animal-biscuit factory, while a mill in Terminus Road, next to the railway, processed animal feeds. In Fishbourne, at the head of the creek, Fred acquired the two water mills in 1918, and used them to make pig-feed, a product marketed as Fishbourne Balanced Cubes.[184]

A corn exchange reborn
Fred Sadler secured the freehold of the Baffins Lane part of the Corn Exchange buildings from George Booth on 2 January 1951, and the conveyance included a covenant restricting him from carrying out any 'noisy, noxious or offensive trade or business', but he was not precluded from carrying on the business of either a corn exchange or of a corn, seed and agricultural merchant.[185]

The company offices were moved from across the road in East Street onto the ground floor of the building, and the upper floors were used for storage. Fred made his office staff work long hours, and they were often going home when the crowds were streaming out of the cinema next door. As the building had not been touched under George Booth's ownership the trading hall, with its stands, was still intact, enabling Fred Sadler to reopen the Corn Exchange for its original purpose. The *Chichester Observer* made no report about the reopening, and nor did

Fred Sadler place an announcement therein to advertise the fact that the corn market was back.

As the city had apparently managed without a corn market for four years the reopening may, on the face of it, seem to have been a strange move, since by this time many corn merchants were driving out to farms and dealing directly with the farmers, cutting out the middle man. The Southern Counties Agricultural Trading Society, a cooperative of local farmers that had an office in Petworth, was also in competition with corn exchanges. However, as the corn market only occupied a small portion of the building, was staffed by Sadler employees and the stand-holders were paying subscriptions and rent, it cost Fred Sadler next to nothing to operate, and so would have generated some profit, however small.

The market was held on alternate Wednesdays, in the afternoon so as not to clash with the cattle market, but David Sadler recalls that business was very slow and those manning the stands spent most of their time talking among themselves as they waited for prospective customers to drift in.

Fred Sadler senior had little respect for bureaucracy, and when in 1958 the building's roof began to leak, threatening his vulnerable stock of grass seed on the top floor, he re-roofed it using asbestos-cement sheeting without first obtaining planning permission. This landed him with a severe reprimand from the city council, but he was used to controversy and not swayed by it.

64 *The last day of trading in Chichester Corn Exchange, 30 June 1966. From left to right are J.P. Heaver, Mr Ellis of Bowyer and Mr Baker of Guildford, Viv Leigh-Thomas of Emsworth and the Isle of Wight, and Mark Jacobs of Heaver's Ratham Mills. The sign over the door is an advertisement for Sheppy fertilisers. The dealers' stands, seen in the background, had been transferred to this room from the main hall in 1927.*

65 *The sale board goes up in Baffins Lane after the closure in 1966, and the buildings quietly await their fate.*

In 1961 Fred Sadler Senior died, aged 94, after a remarkable and colourful life, and the business was carried on by his son Robert and grandson David. The Little London premises were sold in 1964 and became the District Museum, and in 1965 the decision was taken to sell the Corn Exchange buildings and move Sadler's offices to the Terminus Road mill.

The end of the corn market was announced in a letter sent by Sadler's to all stand-holders on 15 December 1965 giving them six months' notice to quit, taking effect from 1 January 1966.[186]

The last day of trading took place on 30 June 1966, but once again the *Chichester Observer* failed to report on it. The Baffins Lane buildings were on the market once more, and the For Sale board erected by Stride & Son advertised it as available for redevelopment to shops and offices. This could be read as implying demolition to create a vacant site, but fortunately this was not to be; the Corn Exchange was set to remain and be faced with another career change. In September the *Chichester Observer* finally woke up to the fact that something had happened in Baffins Lane and put a report in the issue of the 30th of that month under a headline 'Sadlers to move after selling Corn Exchange'. They revealed that the building had been sold for 'well in excess of £40,000'.

Sadler's withdrawal from Baffins Lane might also have sealed the fate of Chichester's corn market but it received another reprieve, this time by D. Combes, who proposed to establish a new corn exchange at Eastgate Hall.

66 *Dudley Combes, pictured in the garden at Oakshade in Market Avenue, c.1950.*

D. Combes, corn and seed merchants

William Combes was born in 1797, and from 1814 was the landlord of the *Anchor* inn in West Street.[187] He was one of the original Corn Exchange shareholders in 1832, investing in five shares, but was not a committee member and his attendance at AGMs was rather sporadic; however, he did attend in 1834 and proposed Henry Sadler as a committee member.[188] William Combes died in 1869 but his son Charles, a West Wittering farmer born in 1822, was elected to the committee in 1874 and regularly attended meetings until 1879. After an absence of three years Charles Combes made his final appearance at the 1883 AGM, and died in September of that year.

The Combes baton then passed to Charles's only son, Conrade Charles Combes, born in 1852, who took on both the family farm, Keynor at Sidlesham, and the family involvement in the Corn Exchange. Conrade* was one of those farmers who had suffered badly from the 1870s agricultural depression, as he described in a memoir written in 1937 when he was 86:

> The seventies were also good, but from then onward things worked against the farmer. Foreign wheat began to pour in, and the labourers were gradually poisoned by agitators. The old hands kept their places, but the young ones gradually passed on to the towns, or other employment until the Boer War when things began to mend.[189]

As a result of this Conrade gave up farming in 1895. He bought 10 shares in the Corn Exchange in 1899 and was elected to the committee that same year, taking the place of the Rev. Mr Rusbridger, who had died. He remained an active member of the committee, and under the changes of 1905 he became a director of the limited company. He increased his shareholding to 19 in 1933 and continued in harness right up to his death in 1946.[190]

Conrade Combes had a son, Dudley, who in 1898 went into business selling hay and straw. He had no yard; instead he bought the hay and straw, trussed it up *in situ* and delivered it direct to the purchasers. He went into partnership with his son Denis, who in 1928 started dealing in corn and feedstuffs from premises at Pound Farm. In about 1922 Dudley had

---

*   This unusual spelling of Conrad occurs on share certificates and in newspaper reports, but I am assured by Pat Combes that his pronunciation of it was conventional.

a new detached house built in Market Avenue that he named Oakshade*
and converted its garage into an office, from whence he ran the business.
In 1936 Combes moved their yard into the Hornet – premises which they
were to buy in 1944 – where Denis took over a saddlery and harness-making
business that had been started by Edward Thomas Harbin, and he ran this
alongside the corn and seed trading.[191]

Dudley Combes first became involved with the Corn Exchange when
his father transferred one of his shares to him in 1937,[192] and at the annual
general meeting of 1940 he became a director and served in this capacity
alongside his father. When Conrade died in 1946 his remaining holding
of 18 shares was transferred to Dudley, who then took a decisive role in the
winding-up of the Corn Exchange Company – it was he who seconded the
proposal to accept Booth's offer to buy the freehold at the special general
meeting on 18 November 1946.

Patrick (Pat) Denis Combes, son of Denis, entered the family business
in 1950, and he opened an additional shop in North Street in 1958 to sell
pets and garden requisites. It was Pat Combes who was to bring about the
second reincarnation of the Chichester Corn Exchange.

A new corn exchange

In April 1966 Pat Combes wrote
to all the 22 standholders and 17
subscribers of the Corn Exchange,
referring to the notice given by Sadler's
and proposing that the business of the
Exchange should continue on alternate
Wednesdays at Eastgate Hall, which
had been provisionally booked for
the purpose.[193] Eastgate Hall, sited
in Market Avenue, had been built
as a Baptist chapel in 1728 and was
acquired by the city council in 1954
for hiring out to the public for the
sort of events that did not warrant the

67 *Eastgate Hall, 2001. It
was subsequently sold by the city
council and converted into a betting
shop. The scruffy building in the
foreground, a public lavatory, has since
been demolished.*

---

*   The house still goes by this name today, but has been extended and converted into
a rest home.

grandeur (or expense) of the Assembly Rooms. As it adjoined the Cattle Market, it was an ideal place to set up the new Corn Exchange.

The letter had a tear-off reply slip that the recipient could use to express an interest and return with an annual subscription of £1 10s. 0d. The response was so good – 28 members having signed up for the first year – that the booking for Eastgate Hall was confirmed, and Pat Combes wrote to the subscribers to say that the first market would take place on Wednesday 13 July 1966 between the hours of 1 and 6 p.m. Yet again the *Chichester Observer* failed to report on the making of an important part of Chichester's marketing history.

Pat Combes acted as voluntary secretary for the venture, which was well supported in its first year and valued by dealers and farmers alike, but membership dropped to 19 in the second year and continued to fall, as those involved ceased trading through retirement or selling-out of their businesses. In 1974 there were only six subscribing members left and so it was decided that the New Corn Exchange should close the following year. One of the businesses that had ceased – at least as far as corn trading was concerned – was D. Combes themselves, who had lost most of their yard in 1974 under a compulsory purchase order made to enable the last section of the ring road, known as Needlemakers, to cut between St Pancras and the Hornet.[194]

The Eastgate Hall Corn Exchange functioned for the last time on Wednesday 21 May 1975, thus ending corn market trading in Chichester for good. Sadly neither Sadler's nor Combes are still in business in Chichester. Sadler's gradually wound down, with Oldacre & Co. acquiring and running Terminus Road Mill, and in 1979 the East Street shop, which had been moved down the road to no. 44 in 1953, became an arcade of shops. D. Combes, on the loss of most of their yard, concentrated on garden supplies and pets in the thatched barn until Pat Combes retired in 1997. The premises are now occupied by Majestic Wines.

EIGHT

'A Great Benefit'
The New Cattle Market 1871-1990

The closure of the beast market in the streets brought about the end of what was widely regarded as 'a great nuisance', as we saw in Chapter Three. However, its closure only came about as the result of a vigorous and hostile campaign by the citizens of Chichester forcing the corporation to build a new beast market away from the city centre. In this chapter we will look at the story of what was called the New Cattle Market, including the events that led up to its creation, which were also somewhat tumultuous.

At war with the populace – again

In 1866 the Common Council finally grasped the beast-market nettle. At a special meeting on 20 November they took the momentous decision to move it to some 'more commodious quarter'.[195] However welcome this news should have been to the populace, when the possible locations for the new venture were announced there ensued what became known as the 'Battle of the Sites'. Five alternative sites for the new market had been proffered:

- Fletcher's Pond to the south east of the city, between the walls and the railway;
- Ballard's Field adjoining the railway to the south of the station;
- the Litten Fields outside the East Walls;
- Habin's Field in the Hornet;
- land off Eastgate Square adjacent to the Baptist chapel.

There were copious differences of opinion, and the correspondence columns of the *West Sussex Gazette* carried many letters airing them. As a result a public meeting – described as 'turbulent' – was called on 19 December 1866 by the mayor, Alderman Robert George Raper,* at which the strongest contenders emerged as Habin's Field and Fletcher's Pond. The council

---

*   Robert George Raper, a revered personage in Chichester, was a partner in the firm of Johnson, Price and Freeland, solicitors. He was knighted in 1886.

then instructed Mr Thomas Hawkesley, an 'eminent (London) engineer', to submit a report giving his views on the matter.[196]

As was so often the case with corporation business, nothing happened quickly, but at a Common Council meeting on 22 October 1867 a letter from Cluttons, the estate agents, was read out regarding the land at Fletcher's Pond, which they were about to auction on behalf of the Ecclesiastical Commissioners. Cluttons offered to postpone the sale in order to allow the corporation time to apply for the necessary parliamentary powers to buy and develop the site, so a sub-committee, consisting of Cllrs Wyatt, Duke, C.T. Halsted, Adames and Henty, was set up to investigate the offer. Eight days later they reported back, but recommended instead using the site off Eastgate Square belonging, among others, to Aldermen Gates and Harbin and William Duke. So vigorous was their recommendation that the Common Council instructed the town clerk to commence parliamentary proceedings at once; the fact that there might be a vested interest by certain councillors in the choice of this site seems to have gone unnoticed. Later at that same meeting the report from Mr Hawkesley was read out. This recommended that the Ballard's Field site be used, as it offered the advantages of being adjacent to the railway from whence a siding could be provided to serve it. Although this idea seemed to have been summarily dismissed by the prior choice of the Eastgate Square site, the meeting agreed that Mr Hawkesley's report would be printed and circulated. The Common Council seemed intent on re-igniting the public confrontation about the choice of site.[197]

At this time the Cattle Market Committee was amalgamated with another to form the Parliamentary, Railway and Cattle Market Committee, chaired by the mayor, in order to take the cattle market project forward.

The 'Battle of the Sites' resumed at the Common Council meeting on 9 November 1867, when Cllr Thomas Smith, a former mayor, objected to the minuting of the proceedings at the previous meeting, pointing out that the vote had been taken by one member of the council who was disqualified by Act of Parliament from so doing as he had not declared a pecuniary interest in the matter.* Furthermore, he remonstrated, the report of 'a distinguished Engineer who had been consulted at the public expense' was refused to be read before a vote on the site of the market was taken, referring of course to Mr Hawkesley. So strong was Cllr Smith's objection that he submitted it in writing, ensuring that it was transcribed verbatim into the minute book. Cllr Smith wrote again in December, and his letter was read out at the meeting of the Common Council on 9 January 1868.

---

* Councillors had, and still have, a legal obligation to declare private interests at the start of each meeting. These interests would be recorded in the minutes. This provided what today would be termed 'transparency'.

68 *An extract from George Loader's 1812 town plan showing the Eastgate Square area. The site chosen for the New Cattle Market is the triangular area covered by trees below the buildings on the south side of the square.*

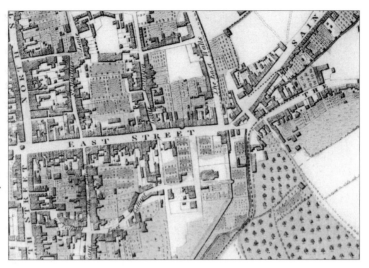

This time he referred to the public meeting held on 13 December* at which a resolution had been carried 'without a discordant vote' disapproving of the recent council proceedings, and suggesting that the parliamentary process be halted 'until arrangements can be made respecting the market more in accordance with the wishes of the Burgesses and ratepayers'. He also pointed out that the councillor who had recommended the Eastgate Square site had failed to find a seconder for his motion in a meeting of nearly 400 persons. He ended the tirade by promising to continue his protest against a project that 'so large a body of my fellow citizens have unequivocally condemned'.

Another public meeting had been held on 8 January 1868, attended by some 300 people, at which two resolutions were carried: Fletcher's Pond was the best site for the majority, and the parliamentary process should be suspended. It is not clear whether this second public meeting had been called by the mayor or (more probably) by Cllr Smith himself as part of his campaign, as it is not recorded in the press, but when he reported on it to the Common Council he also protested against the cost of promoting the bill and declared that he would use his 'utmost endeavours to frustrate attempts to put such costs on Borough rates or the Borough Fund'. Unfortunately for Cllr Smith his Herculean efforts at instilling democracy proved in vain; a vote was carried by 12 votes to five to proceed with the site already decided – i.e. that off Eastgate Square.[198]

The site chosen was a triangular piece of land to the south-east of Eastgate Square, bounded to the west by Snag Lane, a short stretch of adopted road

---

* There is some difference of opinion over the exact date of the public meeting – the minute book records 13 December but the *West Sussex Gazette* in its retrospective report of 11 May 1871 gives it as the 19th inst.

that petered out into a track leading to Kingsham, and on the east by what became the Whyke Lane Twitten.

The Chichester Cattle Market Act

Mr J.J. Johnson QC was engaged to steer the bill through Parliament, and by April 1868 it was before the select committees – with five petitions against it having been received. These were from 'certain ratepayers and inhabitants', William Duke, Mr Hodgskin, the Ecclesiastical Commissioners and the Hon. C.P.F. Berkeley. The bill was supported by 'several witnesses from the City' and the aforementioned Mr Hawkesley, the engineer whose mind about the site had evidently been changed. It cleared select committee stage on 4 May with the Ecclesiastical Commissioners' petition having been withdrawn, those of Messrs Duke and Hodgskin being accommodated and the Hon. Mr Berkeley's having been dismissed.[199]

AN

A C T

(AS AMENDED IN COMMITTEE)

To authorise the Corporation of Chichester to remove the present Cattle Market, and to provide a new Cattle Market, and for other purposes.

WHEREAS by an Act (local) of the forty-seventh year of George the Third, chapter 84, entitled, "An Act to regulate and "improve the Cattle Market, to provide a Market-house, and estab-"lish a market for the sale of butcher's meat and other articles, and "to make other improvements within the City of Chichester, in the "County of Sussex," it was enacted (section 1) that it should and might be lawful for the mayor, aldermen, and citizens of the City of Chichester (in this Act called the Corporation) to hold an open and public market for the sale of live cattle and swine in the East and North Streets of the City, where the same had theretofore been usually holden, and on the same day as the same had been usually holden. And (by section 2) that on the next market-day after the passing of the now-reciting Act, and for ever thereafter, it should and might

69 *The start of the preamble of the Chichester Cattle Market Act, 1868.*

The Act, entitled 'An Act to authorise the Corporation of Chichester to remove the present Cattle Market, and to provide a new Cattle Market, and for other purposes' (or the Chichester Cattle Market Act for short) received royal assent in June 1868 and is in 41 sections.[200] The preamble begins by reciting the 1807 Act that had regulated the old market and authorised the new Market House, and then goes on to give justifications for this new Act, including

> AND WHEREAS … the market has of late largely increased, and the holding thereof in those streets, public thoroughfares, and vacant spaces occasions great obstruction and inconvenience to the inhabitants of the City, and it is expedient that provision be made for the discontinuance and removal of such market, and that the Corporation be authorised to provide a New Cattle Market, and to purchase and acquire lands for that purpose.

The powers granted enabled the corporation to purchase the land compulsorily, construct the market, build a new road, divert the River

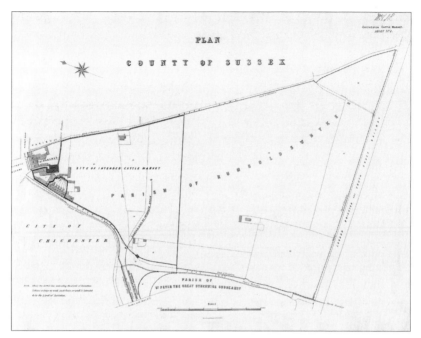

70 *An extract from the deposited plans that accompanied the Chichester Cattle Market Bill, showing the area to be purchased compulsorily and the start of the route of the new road that would become Market Road. It can be seen that the limits of deviation extend as far as the railway, but the land purchased did not actually extend as far as that.*

Lavant into a culvert and discontinue the beast market in the streets. It made the subsequent selling of 'cattle beasts or animals' in the streets unlawful and punishable by a fine of £10, and also authorised the corporation to establish a set of rules covering the regulation of the market. The Act gave schedules of the tolls that should be levied within the market.

71 *Schedule 'A' of the Chichester Cattle Market Act setting out the tolls on animal sales. The figures on the extreme left-hand edge of the page are the line reference numbers and not some obscure subdivision of a penny!*

14   *Chichester Cattle Market.*

The SCHEDULES referred to in the foregoing Act.

SCHEDULE A.

CATTLE MARKET TOLLS.

	£	s.	d.
For each horse, mare or pony, not exceeding - -	0	0	6 5
For each mare with a foal, including the foal, not exceeding - - - - - -	0	0	9
For each foal not exceeding - - - - -	0	0	4
For each ass or mule, not exceeding - - -	0	0	3
For each bull, not exceeding - - - -	0	1	0 10
For each bullock, cow, steer, or heifer, whether tied or not; and if tied including use of tie, not exceeding -	0	0	4
For each calf, not exceeding - - - -	0	0	2
For each sheep, ram, lamb, pig or goat, not exceeding	0	0	1
For every stallion or entire horse, and for every other animal not before-named in this schedule, brought into the market for sale or for show, not exceeding -	0	1	0

And the above tolls to be payable for each beast or animal for each day or part of a day in which the same is placed in the market, whether for sale or not and whether sold or not.

AUCTION TOLLS.

For each horse, mare, pony, bull, bullock, cow or other beast or animal offered for sale by auction, and whether sold or not, (and in addition to the toll above-mentioned,) not exceeding - - - - - | 0 | 1 | 0

Under construction

With the will of Parliament behind them, if not necessarily that of the populace at large, the corporation engaged Mr Hawkesley to prepare plans and specifications for the new Cattle Market and served compulsory purchase orders on the row of cottages, 3 to 9 Snag Lane, on the western edge of the site, that can be seen in Fig. 69. The compulsory purchase was, naturally, unpopular, and claims amounting to £1,886 18s. 4d. were received, which had to be referred to arbitration for a decision.

With his design approved, Mr Hawkesley was appointed engineer for the works in March 1869 at a fee of five per cent of the construction costs. The package of works, estimated at £15,000, included the diversion of the River Lavant into a culvert, but the construction of the new road – Market Road – was an extra estimated at £1,500. The corporation took out a mortgage of £13,200 towards the funding of their new venture.

Tenders were invited for two contracts: no. 2 for the ironwork for the pens and standings and no. 1 for everything else. The contracts were awarded in April 1870, Frederick Furniss from Langstone in Hampshire winning no. 1 at £5,477 13s. 3½d. and Joseph Cliff & Co. of Bradford winning no. 2 at £2,107 4s. 3½d. Interestingly one firm that did not tender for the

72 *The turning of the first sod of the new Cattle Market on 7 April 1870. In the centre can be seen the Mayor of Chichester Alderman Samuel Merricks, resplendent in his robes, with the spade leaning against the wheelbarrow. To the right are the ranks of the contractor's workforce. In the background, beyond the mulberry tree, can be seen the rear of properties in Eastgate Square.*

ironwork contract was Halsted & Sons of Chichester. Halsted's foundry, between East Street and North Pallant, was run by Charles Townsend (C.T.) Halsted. C.T. Halsted was a councillor, had been Mayor of Chichester in 1858 and was also a director of the Chichester Old Bank, but although his proximity to the site should have offered savings on transportation costs, perhaps his tendering might have been seen as a rather blatant conflict of interest.[201] By 5 April all the land had been acquired save for the Snag Lane cottages, and Mr Lambert had been appointed as clerk of works. The corporation was ready for the off.

The commencement of the works was marked on 7 April 1870 by the traditional ceremony of turning the first sod. This was performed by the mayor, Alderman Samuel Merricks, and the great and the good of the city gathered at noon to witness it. A platform was set up under a mulberry tree at the northern end of the site and the mayor thoughtfully provided a barrel of beer for the workmen who had joined the throng. This doubtless helped to take their minds off the numerous pompous addresses given before the mayor stepped forward to say: 'It devolves upon me, as Mayor of the City, to turn the first sod of the New Cattle Market. I do this with much pleasure, heartily wishing all success to the undertaking and sincerely trusting it may be an increasing source of prosperity to our ancient city.' With that the clerk of works, Mr Lambert, handed the mayor a spade with which he duly turned the first sod, breaking a bottle of champagne over it, transferring it to the wheelbarrow and then wheeling it along a plank. The company (save, of course, for the workmen who were left with their beer) then repaired to the Council House where luncheon, served by Messrs Ballard of the *Dolphin Hotel*, was taken at 2 p.m. Among the many speeches was one by Cllr Thomas Smith, who proposed a toast to the Cattle Market and said that his differences over the site were now in the past, and he believed that the new market would prove 'a great benefit'. It fell to Cllr C.T. Halsted to propose a toast to the engineer, Mr Hawkesley, who, being unable to attend, unfortunately did not hear it, but his clerk of works responded on his behalf.[202] From the number of toasts drunk, a merry time was obviously had by all in marking this auspicious occasion.

With the jollifications over, work proceeded apace and just under a year later, on 31 March 1871, the Markets Committee was able to submit a favourable progress report to the Common Council:

> With respect to Contract No. 2 your committee have much pleasure in reporting that Messrs Cliff & Co. have executed the work to their entire satisfaction and Mr Hawkesley has expressed himself as being equally well satisfied … Your Committee have to report that certain matters still remain to be settled with Mr Furniss [the main contractor] which they have no doubt will be speedily concluded.

There is an implication that all was not well with the main contract, and indeed Mr Furniss had submitted a claim that was later settled at £118. The committee went on to recommend that a shed containing accommodation for 'settling places' should be erected against one of the walls and tabled a plan of the same for approval by the council. They also reported that 'closets' were about to be erected around the market.[203]

At that Common Council meeting of 31 March 1871 it was agreed that, as the works were so well advanced, public notice could be given about the discontinuation of the existing street market and the opening of the new facility. It was recommended that the New Cattle Market be opened on 10 May, be held on alternate Wednesdays and that bylaws covering the conduct of the market should be drawn up under the terms of the 1868 Act. It was also recommended by the Markets Committee that the collection of tolls should be kept in the corporation's own hands (i.e. not leased out as hitherto), and Mr Tiffin was put forward as collector on a two per cent commission.[204]

The notices were duly placed in the *West Sussex Gazette* of 4 May 1871, one advising that the new market would be open for public use on 10 May 1871 and giving the hours of business, and another publishing the 15 bylaws for the regulation of the market. Beneath these two notices was another, advertising the 'Opening Dinner for the New Cattle Market' that was to be held on the same day at the *Dolphin Hotel* in the presence of the Duke of Richmond and the mayor and corporation of Chichester. Tickets were to be had at 4s., 'including waiter'.

The opening

The opening ceremony on 10 May 1871 was no less grand than that of the turning of the first sod, but unfortunately for the mayor, Robert

73 *The Mayor and Corporation at the opening of the New Cattle Market, 10 May 1871, with the gates onto Eastgate Square open wide. The city crest can be seen emblazoned on the gates. The* Hampshire Telegraph *reported that the photograph was taken by Mr J.L. Russell, who 'was perched with his assistants' at the window of a building opposite.*

George Raper, and the accompanying dignitaries it took place at the rather antisocial hour of 5 a.m. The report in the *West Sussex Gazette*, published the following day, took up over two feet of column inches in its characteristically effusive style. Here is a flavour:

> The morning was clear and bright and some time before the hour a small crowd had collected round the Eastgate entrance gate and behind this barrier the Mayor and several members of the corporation were in waiting. Just as the St Pancras clock struck five, the Mayor and Town Clerk and members of the Council present advanced to the gate and the declared the market open. The key was turned in the lock and the flood poured in. There was a good sprinkling of all classes about and the pens seemed to be the subject of considerable criticism … The Mayor and the Corporation members present (Messrs Habin, Halsted, Gadd, Collins, Allen Molesworth and Merricks) were attentive in seeing to the wants of the dealers, and after a morning or two no doubt but that the New Cattle Market will be 'liked all round'. The site is very open and it is likely that after a time sheds will be erected.

At six o'clock the assembled company repaired to St Pancras Church for a special service at which the rector, the Rev. F.F. Tracy, delivered an address, taking as his text Proverbs iii, verse 9: 'Honour the Lord with thy substance and with the first fruits of their increase.' The attendance at the market was reckoned to be above the average for the former street market and prices were good, but some thought the site was rather bleak.[205]

In the afternoon, after the market had closed, the mayor, dignitaries and paying guests repaired to the *Dolphin Hotel* for the opening dinner. This was attended by around 150, including the city's MP, Lord Henry Lennox, the Duke's brother. There were, inevitably, numerous speeches, opened by the Duke of Richmond, who was greeted with 'a tremendous round of applause'. One of the guests was Canon Swainson, who had so vigorously headed the campaign to close down the beast market in the streets, and he proposed the toast on behalf of the Bishop of Chichester and the cathedral clergy. The mayor's lengthy speech set out the history of the New Cattle Market (or rather his version of it), and included something by way of a corporate acknowledgement of guilt at having ignored the public protests about the beast market in the streets:

> Well, we paid only courteous [*sic*] attention to those complaints and continued to keep it on, thinking the pressure should come from without and not from the civic body. At last matters were sufficiently ripe for a resolution to be passed by the Corporation for the removal of the market from the streets of the city.

He went on to cite the 'Battle of the Sites', but opined that

> before the anniversary of the opening of the market is celebrated, the
> verdict of the public will be 'The site was the right one: the market is
> growing into the finest out of London, and long may it exist for the
> prosperity of the city and those who frequent it.

His speech was greeted with 'loud cheers'.[206]

The New Cattle Market

The six-acre site, as can be seen from Fig. 75, was laid out with numbered
pens of various sizes. Formed of cast-iron posts and rails and dispersed
about wide aisles, they could accommodate 4,000 fat and 7,000 store sheep,
1,500 pigs, 60 fat and 220 lean calves, 150 fat bullocks and 1,300 store
cattle. Some of the latter could be tethered to iron rings set in the walls.
These rings were carried by shanks that passed through the brickwork and
secured by patress plates on the other side, where they can still be seen in

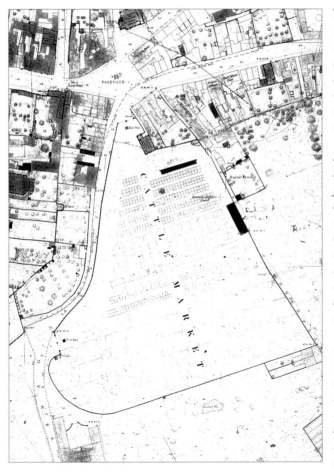

74 *An extract from the
1875 Ordnance Survey at
1:500 scale showing the
layout of the New Cattle
Market three years after
opening. It can be seen
that there are only two
buildings, those marked
'offices' at the north end
and the refreshment shed
against the east wall,
justifying the complaints
about the site being rather
bleak. At the north end
of the site it can be seen
that the new market
had engulfed the Baptist
chapel, so independent
access to it was made via a
walled twitten to its east.
There are toll booths at
both entrances. Outside the
walls to the south-east of
the site is the Caledonian
Iron Works, run by Peter
Buchan, which made
agricultural machinery.
It closed in 1905 but the
buildings still stand.*

75 *Relics of the Cattle Market: left, some of the rings in the east wall; right, some of the patress plates securing the rings, visible from the Whyke Lane twitten at the time of writing.*

the Whyke Lane twitten. The horse market was held at the south end of the site and featured a 'trying ground', where dealers could show off their stock in trade.[207]

There were two entrances to the market site, one at the north end facing Eastgate Square and the other at the south end off the new road, but they failed to impress the *West Sussex Gazette* reporter who felt they had 'nothing striking' about them. The gates each carried a cast-iron city crest. After the opening in 1871 two nearby public houses in Eastgate Square changed their names, that on the corner of Market Road becoming the *Cattle Market Inn* and that on the south side (at no. 16) the *Market Tavern*. Both these have long since closed and became shops, but beneath the fascia of no. 16 lurks the old pub name in glazed tiles, which emerges from time to time when the shop changes hands and is refurbished.

The new road, named (what else?) Market Road,* cut through from the south-east corner of the market to Basin Road; it was not completed until April 1872 and was declared a public highway on opening. It served to link the market with the railway station, where a large cattle dock was provided for animals arriving by train.

In business

In July 1871 the Cattle Market Committee was proudly able to report on the receipts for first four markets held:

---

* The north end of Snag Lane became part of Market Road, but its remaining section remained a track until, in the late 19th century, it was made up to become Stirling Road as far as the railway. In the 20th century the portion of Market Road beyond the junction with Snag Lane was renamed Market Avenue, presumably to make the new houses being built along it more marketable.

76 *One of the cast-iron city crests that used to adorn the entrance gates to the New Cattle Market.*

10 May	£53	1s.	7d. (the first day)
24 May	£77	18s.	5d.
7 June	£46	19s.	8d.
21 June	£57	15s.	7d.

From this they were confidently able to opine that 'it therefore appears that sufficient tolls will probably be received to meet the annual sum required from the principal amount raised under the powers of the Act and the interest thereon'. The final account was being prepared, and they anticipated that the full £15,000 authorised would be expended.[208]

As the lack of basic facilities was so obviously unpopular, the council agreed to award a contract to Mr Hennett to provide refreshments for £20 a year, commencing on 1 January 1872. He operated out of what was inelegantly termed a 'refreshment shed' that they had just built against the east wall of the site. Deliberations about providing covered accommodation for the market took place at many a Common Council meeting throughout 1872 and 1873, and a recommendation for the provision of 'better protection, comfort and convenience of the frequenters of the cattle market' was even made by the mayor, John Caffin. Despite this it can be seen that by 1874, when the Ordnance Survey mapped the site, absolutely nothing had been provided, so all business had to be carried out in the open in all weathers.

The first year of trading generated an income of £1,027 17s. 1d. against expenditure of £1,102 10s. 1d., so the venture was not yet in profit, but it needs to be pointed out that £1,012 10s. of the expenditure was incurred servicing the loans.[209]

77 *An early view of the north end of the New Cattle Market looking towards Eastgate Square. The two gentlemen are, perhaps, negotiating the sale of the sheep in the pens. To the right can be seen the Baptist chapel that had found itself engulfed by the new market. Fortunately for worshippers the market was closed on Sundays.*

It has been remarked that Cllr C.T. Halsted, who ran the iron foundry in East Pallant, had not tendered for any of the work in the construction of the market, but he did finally make his mark on it in 1873 when he was awarded the £45 job of altering 22 of the pig pens in order to prevent the escape of (presumably small) pigs.

The first superintendent and keeper of the market, William Tuffin, resigned in September 1873 and he was replaced by Arthur Pratt, who took on the role as an extension of his duties as superintendent of police, for which he was to be paid an extra £10 a year. One improvement made at this time was in the matter of toll collection. In order to speed up the removal of animals at the end of the day it was decided to collect the tolls when the beasts entered the market, so toll booths were erected at both entrances, each manned by a collector and an assistant.[210] These booths are marked on the Ordnance Survey map of 1875.

The market was highly successful, with traders coming from all over the south and west of England by train. As the *Hampshire Telegraph* reported in its issue of 28 May 1881, it was felt that with the new Chichester to Midhurst railway about to open, even more of the agricultural district would be opened up and that accordingly the need to hold the market weekly instead of fortnightly was perceived. Indeed, the *Hampshire Telegraph* opined, there was 'no reason to doubt that a weekly market would be as successful as the fortnightly one has proved'. This matter duly came up at the Common Council meeting on 31 May, where the committee made the recommendation to increase the frequency to weekly and a council resolution was taken to introduce it. Strangely, despite the resolution, the cattle market remained fortnightly until 1893.

Plagues

Markets are vulnerable to the effects of animal diseases, and a special cattle diseases committee was set up to manage the problem under the watchful eye of the clerk of the peace to the county. There were several outbreaks of the devastating foot and mouth disease in the south of England after 1877, and for that of December 1881 an Order in Council was issued closing markets in Sussex and Surrey – but not in Hampshire. The only exception was for animals sold under special licence, which had to be slaughtered within six days of sale. In view of this the decision was taken to close the Chichester market completely from 4 January 1882, as previous experience had shown that it was impracticable to keep it open under such stringent conditions. It reopened the following March, only to be closed again in another outbreak at the end of the year.[211]

The special committee's experience was extended in August 1886 when swine fever broke out in Sussex, but they managed to avoid closure of the market by introducing a complex marking system to identify pigs being brought in and out, so as to ensure that they were slaughtered and not sold on as store livestock.[212]

Improvements

The first stage of providing covered accommodation began in May 1875 when Mr Willshire was awarded a contract by the corporation to provide a lean-to shed, 50 yards in length and 12 feet in width, against the east wall. It was situated to the south of the refreshment shed, which, under the same contract, was provided with five new windows. The following year the paving of the pens with Fareham blue bricks was commenced, but the paving was a long process not to be completed until the early 20th century, so one can only assume that a visit to the market on a wet day was closely akin to a day on the farm – a whiff of *rus in urbe* perhaps.[213]

The 1868 Act allowed for the fact that beasts might be sold by auction as well as private treaty, and an additional toll of up to 1s. could be charged for such sales. By 1878 the number of auctioned transactions was increasing, so the Cattle Market Committee decided to dedicate the area in the south-west corner of the market to auctions and pave it for the purpose. Animals for sale by auction now had to be declared as such on entry, and an additional toll of 4d. per beast was levied.[214]

This new condition did not prove popular, and in 1880 one firm of auctioneers, Messrs Hobgen, founded in 1864, decided to hold their auctions outside the market to avoid the tolls. For this they received a sharp rebuke from the corporation, who informed them that their actions infringed the Cattle Market Act and therefore they must conduct future sales within the market. Hobgen's duly obeyed, and later that year negotiated a three-year lease of part of the south-west corner at £25 a year and, at their own expense, erected a shed over part of it. They had, literally, cornered the market – and provided the luxury of shelter from the rain into the bargain. The following year another long-established firm of Chichester auctioneers and estate agents, Wyatt & Sons (of whom more anon) applied to enter the auction area, and they were granted the same terms as the Hobgen brothers.

Although not adjacent to the railway, the Cattle Market was not far from it, and the committee felt that a rail connection would be an advantage. As such they resolved at their meeting of 22 March 1881 to write to the London Brighton & South Coast Railway suggesting the provision of 'a siding into the Cattle Market ... for the greater convenience of getting stock into and from the market'. As is so often the case with corporation business the outcome of the idea is not recorded. Suffice to say it did not happen, and doubtless the LB&SCR in its response pointed out that it was more than a case of 'a siding' since, being outside station limits, it would have entailed a fully signalled connection from the main line with a new signal-box and cross-over – a great expense for a line that would be used only fortnightly. Although the Chichester Market branch line was destined to become an interesting might-have-been, a lesser investment by the corporation resulted in the planting of trees around the perimeter of the site, commenced in May 1883.[215]

The Cattle Market Committee had maintained its separate existence for 20 years, but in 1885, in an early form of streamlining it was amalgamated with other bodies to become the Highways, Paving, Cattle Market and Cattle Diseases Committee, a new and much wider broom.

Charles Stride and his battle

So successful was Hobgen's dedicated auction area that in 1890 they added another span to their building and paved the area beneath it at their own expense. That same year, however, a formidable competitor appeared on the scene in the form of Mr Charles Stride.

Charles Stride was a local farmer who in 1890 decided to extend his business by setting up as an auctioneer, thus founding the well-respected firm that was to become Stride & Son, still in business today. Stride's were to shape the way the Cattle Market was run right up to its closure 100 years later – but the relationship got off to an acrimonious start with a vigorous battle waged against both Hobgen's and the corporation.

The battle commenced in June 1890 when the committee received a letter from Messrs Stride, Waddington and Rusbridger (addressed from Manor Farm, Lavant) giving their proposal for selling livestock by auction in the cattle market. The committee duly sent a copy of the market rules, but the three immediately mounted a challenge, wanting to auction livestock in the pens rather than in the auction area – and without paying the auction toll. The letter went on to point out that they had 500 store sheep promised for auction, but the existing auction area in the market was too limited in space to accommodate them. They ended by requesting two rows of pens for this venture.

The committee dug their heels in over relaxing the tolls but resolved to look at extending the area set aside for auctions. Charles Stride and his associates attended the committee meeting of 11 July to put their case, but the committee decided they needed to consult the existing tenant-auctioneers – Hobgen's and Wyatt's – so that they could put their case forward. Wyatt's were unable to attend that meeting, but sent in a letter pointing out that although they did not know the details of Stride's proposal they had been auctioning livestock before the move of the beast market from the streets and had attended every market day since, and duly paid their tolls. Hobgen's did attend, however, and made a strong case against

Stride's proposal, feeling that it would be an infringement of their lease. They stressed that they had erected and paid for buildings, and expected that other auctioneers should be subjected to the same conditions. Then, in something of a side-swipe at the corporation, they pointed out that they frequently had to turn away stock owing to lack of space and that 'the great attraction which has rendered our sales so successful is the possession of covered buildings … the enterprise was ours, it is not right that we should be deprived of it'.[216]

Hobgen's powerful oration caused the committee to write to Charles Stride informing him that his proposal could not be entertained – first round to Hobgen's. At their meeting of 8 August the committee considered two more letters they had received. The first was from Stride, Waddington and Rusbridger, offering to pay an annual rent for a portion of the pens in lieu of auction tolls. This was swiftly rejected. The next letter was from Hobgen's, who reported seeing an advertisement in the *West Sussex Gazette* stating that Charles Stride was preparing to hold auctions in the Cattle Market, and queried whether the corporation had sanctioned this infringement of their lease: they had not.

Obviously fearing a long and bitter battle, the committee agreed in September to set aside 31 pens for auction sales, and notices were placed advising of this. Charles Stride appeared to have made a gain. Hobgen's, though, observing another of Stride's adverts in October, wrote again to the corporation asking what action was being taken and warning that in the event of Stride's sales continuing they would be 'compelled to take such steps as will secure to us those privileges which we are justly entitled to under our agreement'. Meanwhile Stride, Waddington & Rusbridger had written again, this time advising the committee that they intended to hold a sale of horses just outside the market walls in Mr Sayer's yard in Caledonian Road,* and asking whether such a sale would incur tolls.

Nettled by both letters, the committee instructed the town clerk to write to Hobgen's denying responsibility for Stride's action, and to Charles Stride to say that market tolls *would* be payable and that sales outside the market 'will lead to much inconvenience and might be deemed to be a disturbance to the market'. The legal justification for both these assumptions seems shaky, but the sergeant of police was asked to attend the horse sale to take note of what happened, and be prepared to give evidence if required.[217] The battle was intensifying.

In their next move Charles Stride and his cronies joined forces with Fred Pitt, a farmer from East Broyle whom R. Rider Haggard was later to interview, to form the Chichester Auction Company, under which

---

* James Sayer was a coal and builders' merchant who had opened a yard in the new Caledonian Road to the south of the Cattle Market. He also had premises in Southgate.

name they wrote to the corporation in December 1890 from an address at 47 East Street. In this missive they challenged both the corporation's right to demand tolls for an auction held outside the Cattle Market and the presumption that such a sale would constitute a disturbance:

> We desire to work harmoniously with the Corporation and they should be alive to the fact that our interests are identical to their own ... Auctions are becoming more and more the order of the day ... [there is] no doubt that all stock in the district will be sold by auction in the near future.

The letter ended with the undertaking that if they were to be put on the same terms as Hobgen's they would not hold any more sales outside the Cattle Market. The committee's response on 2 January 1891 was simply to extend the hours for auctions to 6 p.m. and to notify the auction company that they would take action 'to protect the interests of citizens' should any further sales by them be arranged. In April 1891 the auction company advertised a second horse sale in Sayer's Yard, so the enraged corporation sought the advice of learned counsel. Another meeting was held with the auction company, at which they once again denied causing a disturbance but put forward a proposal for the committee's consideration. At their meeting of 17 July the committee honed the said proposal into a form that could be put to the council for approval:

> On or before 1 January 1893 the Corporation will discontinue charges for auction sales, charge only tolls and allow auction sales on alternate Wednesdays.
> The Auction Company will not hold any sales outside the market.
> The Auction Company will pay auction tolls in addition to market tolls until the discontinuance of the auction tolls.

Counsel's advice had been to accept the terms, abolish auction tolls for everybody and consider allowing a number of auctions to take place at the

78 *A letter heading for the Chichester Auction Co. Ltd, listing Messrs Stride, Waddington and Rusbridger. It is dated 1895, by which time they had moved to 63 East Street.*

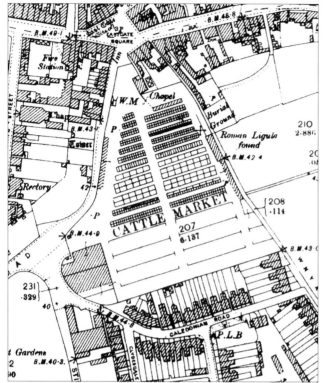

79 *An extract from the 1896 edition of the Ordnance Survey at 1:2500 scale showing how the facilities had developed. Hodgen's auction sheds are in the south-west corner, adjacent to the southern entrance, the corporation's long lean-to shed is next to the refreshment shed against the east wall, and another has been erected against the west wall next to Market Road. Outside the walls the area to the south has been developed as Caledonian Road.*

same time. The end of the battle was in sight, but unfortunately another challenge came, this time from a Mr Henry Smith, an auctioneer from Brighton, who advertised a sale of horses and carriages to take place in October in the yard of the *Globe* at Southgate. Once again hackles rose, and the town clerk was instructed to write to Mr Smith declaring his sale to be a disturbance and that proceedings would be taken. The sergeant of police was urged to take steps to avoid a breach of the law.

The final move was made in October 1891 when a deputation consisting of Messrs Stride, Pitts, Waddington and Rusbridger met the committee, and gave an assurance that they would hold no more outside sales once the auction tolls were suspended. The auction tolls duly ceased on 9 November 1891, and the 16-month battle was over.[218]

Peace returns

With the battle over, Stride's held regular auctions alongside the Hobgen brothers and Wyatt and Co., and the Cattle Market settled down to a quieter life. The new recreation ground in New Park had been added to the committee's remit in 1888 and that was now taking up most of their time. In July 1892 the Cattle Market received a visit from a travelling inspector from the Board of Agriculture, a man blessed with the name of

Mr A. Chichester. While he praised the way the market was run generally, he criticised the fact that the places where cattle stood were not paved, since 'regulations' required such areas to be washed down after use. As a result the city surveyor was instructed to prepare a scheme for completing the paving of the market.

Another challenge to the way the market was run arose in May 1893, when a petition was received by the committee from nine 'regular attendants' at the market, requesting that a number of pens be reserved for use in the manner of the stands at the Corn Exchange, for which they would be prepared to pay £1 a year. Their leader was Mr Haines of Lavant, who apologised for the soiled state of the paper – which resulted from its having been handed round for signature during the market! The committee agreed to an experimental period of three months but restricted the number of pens to ten. Unfortunately for Mr Haines the experiment was terminated the following August, as it had not been found to work to the corporation's satisfaction.

Back in 1881 the Common Council had agreed to increase the frequency of the market to weekly, but for some unrecorded reason this was not implemented. However, at their meeting of 11 May 1893 the committee proposed to revive the idea, but straightaway received from Messrs Hobgen a petition signed by 38 farmers and 47 butchers against the move. Despite this opposition the committee resolved to open the market every Wednesday from September, and the town clerk was instructed to post public notices

80 *The Cattle Market in the 1890s, with sheep in the pens. The sign on the tree denotes Alley No. 10. The narrow aisles between the pens were called alleys while the wider ones between the blocks were rather grandly termed avenues.*

about the same. Charles Stride, still trading as the Chichester Auction Company, wrote to the corporation in October complaining of poor business at the weekly markets, saying that 'something more than simply opening the gates will be needed to establish a weekly market in Chichester'. He complained that the tenants had had to do all the advertising and as a result he would be reverting to a fortnightly market; and trusted that his company would not be charged for the alternate weeks when he was not there. Charles Stride was obviously not the only one to feel this way, since the weekly markets were suspended in September 1894. From then until 1952, the market remained fortnightly.[219]

Chichester Corporation undertook another reshuffle of their committees at the end of December 1896, and the management of the Cattle Market was, with somewhat baffling logic, thrown in with school attendance and allotments. The clumsy name of the new body was the School Attendance, Cattle Market and Recreation Ground Committee and Allotment Managers. From now on the market seldom commanded the committee's attention, and most of their time was taken up with bringing the parents of truants to justice. Perhaps it was felt that the Cattle Market had reached its zenith and could run itself.[220]

The coupling of school attendance and markets inevitably proved unworkable, and in November 1898 another reshuffle found the market's business transferred to a new Highways, Paving, Lighting, Canal and Cattle Market Committee – an apparently more logical combination of functions. At their meeting of 25 August 1899 the city accountant proudly reported the number of markets that had yielded in excess of £40 in tolls: three in 1896, none in 1897 and three in 1899. Furthermore the market held on 12 August 1899 had featured 8,967 entries (of which 7,852 were sheep), yielding tolls of £43 10s. 11d. 'This', the accountant went on to report, 'is the largest market since July 15 1896.'[221] The 19th century was coming to a successful end as far as the New Cattle Market was concerned.

New century
The new century got off to a bad start, with a suspected case of swine fever being detected in February 1900, resulting in a closure of the market to pigs. Another outbreak a year later was dealt with by cleansing and limewashing both the pig pens and the carts coming into the market. Another year on, in February 1902, the town clerk had to tell the committee that an 'unwholesome' animal had been brought into the market; the superintendent had called in a vet who diagnosed the sheep in question to be suffering from tuberculosis. The owner of the unfortunate animal was given a stern warning and the town clerk was instructed to produce posters warning the general public not to bring 'unwholesome animals' into the market.[222]

81 *A postcard of the Cattle Market, postmarked 1911. The view is looking north-north-east, towards Eastgate Square. The railway-like building in the right background houses the market offices and it can be seen that the trees planted around the perimeter in 1883 have matured nicely and softened the bleak landscape a little.*

We met H. Rider Haggard and his 1901 survey of British agriculture in Chapter One. As part of his researches into Sussex he visited Chichester on market day, and wrote of his experiences:

> Chichester market is held once a fortnight upon Wednesdays. I attended it, and although the day was particularly wretched, with pouring rain and a gale of north-east wind, I can well believe that its repute as the best in England, Norwich excepted, is no exaggeration of the facts. The company was large and there was a great deal of stock on sale, some of which fetched good prices. Thus two pens of lambs belonging to Mr Pitts, whose farm I described, which had been dropped before Christmas, were knocked down at 43s. and 43s. 6d. apiece for butchering purposes … In a field adjoining the market a patent American hay loader, called the 'Ohio', was exemplifying its merits by picking up wet straw thickly strewn about the grass and depositing it upon the wagon to which it was affixed.

Although the climatic conditions were far from ideal, he had at least picked a day when no unwholesome animals were abroad. Rider Haggard had also met the redoubtable Charles Stride, describing his as one of the most interesting interviews he had had in the district. He wrote that Mr Stride was a well-known Chichester auctioneer who also had a large farm of both his own and tenanted land.* Probably unaware of the way in which Charles Stride had gained his entry to the Cattle Market, Rider Haggard, with masterly understatement, opined that he was 'evidently a gentleman who thinks for himself'.[223]

Stride's empire grows

Charles Stride, having made peace with the Cattle Market Committee, began to increase his foothold in the market. In January 1903 he was granted a lease of a site in the south-east corner of the market next to the wall against Whyke Lane for the sale of stock and store cattle. The protracted negotiations were doubtless not easy for the corporation, and Charles Stride was permitted to have a covered sale ring and weighbridge on the site. That same year the Chichester Auction Company changed its name to Stride & Son; its office remained at 63 East Street, which had been the auction company's address since 1894.

Mr Stride was obviously impatient to move in to his new market accommodation, for he kept pressing the corporation and twice had to be put off as the work was not complete. He finally began trading from the new area on 27 April 1904, but no sooner had he done so he applied to lease yet more of the site – his empire was growing.[224]

Unfortunately Mr Stride's use of the new facilities quickly lead to a dispute over the cleansing of the same; he refusing to do it, claiming it to be the council's responsibility. As the Board of Agriculture had issued to the corporation edicts about cleanliness following recent outbreaks of disease, the problem had to be nipped in the

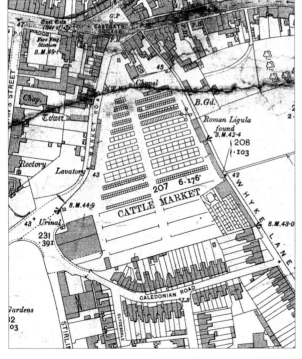

82 *The layout of the Cattle Market as shown on the 1912 OS map at 1:2500 scale. Stride & Son's premises are in the south-east corner of the site. There are covered cattle sheds against the wall next to Whyke Lane and a sale ring in front of the pens. The Hobgen brothers were still occupying the two sheds in the opposite corner.*

---

*   These farms were Warehead (Halnaker) and Lidsey.

bud, so a small deputation was sent by the committee to meet Mr Stride and put him right as to his responsibilities. Needless to say Mr Stride used the meeting to his advantage, undertaking to cleanse the site and comply with all regulations 'without question' provided the corporation would lay on a suitable water supply. He went on to press the importance to him of obtaining the extra land, and then requested the right to hold extra sales on non-market days. Once again the corporation agreed to his requests, and the extension to his premises was carried out in 1905.

Stride's rivals, Wyatt and Sons and the Hobgen brothers, were still active at this time, being authorised from time to time to hold extra sales on non-market days. Indeed, extra sales on non-market days by all three resident auctioneers were to become a common feature of the market.[225]

Disorder in the camp

The corporation's committee structure was changed yet again in November 1904, with the Cattle Market now being controlled by the Highway, Paving, Cattle Market and Labour Committee, and one of the first challenges of this new committee was that of the behaviour of unwanted intruders. Back in July that year the superintendent had been instructed to see that dogs were not allowed to stray and get out of control, and his attention was called to 'the behaviour of boys in order that they may not worry the stock'. In June 1905 two boys were caught damaging a store in the market, and the father of one offered to pay for the repairs in lieu of his wayward son being prosecuted. When the committee debated this the resolution that both boys be summonsed was lost; instead the boys were ordered to appear before them. On the following 3 July Mrs Gardner and Mr Balchin duly accompanied their errant sons to the meeting, where, having convinced the committee that the boys had been suitably punished and that they would make good the damage, it was decided that charges would not be pressed.[226]

Unfortunately for the committee the problems with dogs and boys were added to by the misdemeanours of their own staff. In September 1907 the market superintendent resigned and the post was offered to William Hopkins, one of the toll collectors. Hopkins, however, withdrew his application so the second-choice applicant, Barrett Thrift, was appointed instead. This soon proved to have been a mistake, for in February 1908 Thrift had to be reprimanded for not handing over money he had received for limewashing carts, a transgression that obviously proved to be only the tip of the iceberg – for the committee resolved to dismiss him in March. The job was once again offered to Hopkins, who this time accepted.[227]

Yet more trouble followed in November 1910. Although the corporation was still steadily paving the market, the rate of progress did not satisfy the Board of Agriculture, who, following yet another incidence of disease, ordered the corporation to complete the job. The city surveyor estimated that concreting the remaining unpaved areas would cost £1,616, so it was agreed to proceed at once and borrow the money to fund the exercise. A week later they changed their collective mind and wrote to the Board of Agriculture seeking permission to extend the time for completing the work in order to avoid taking out the loan. With clever civil service evasion the board declined to grant the extra time requested, but stated that if it were completed within the next five years they would not press the matter.

Further problems arose with boys, this time with some unidentified ones who threw stones over the market wall, breaking windows in Mr Holden's greenhouse in Caledonian Road. This caused the committee to instruct the superintendent to keep boys out of the market altogether, which, given their amazing ability to climb walls as an alternative to using the gates, would have been a tall order to carry out.[228]

The First World War

Not long after war broke out the committee received reports that 'the military' were stabling horses in the market sheds and bringing motor vehicles onto the site. Instead of showing the public spirit of pulling

83 *Another early 20th-century view of the Cattle Market, showing sheep in pens and, in the left background, the mulberry tree that had featured in the ceremony of the cutting of the first sod. This photograph must predate the 1910 ban on boys, judging by the number of them in the assembled multitude.*

84 *The catalogue for a major wartime sale of Southdown sheep by Stride & Son, August 1916.*

together for the war effort, the corporation decided to charge the army 3d. per day for every vehicle parked in the market and to hold them responsible for any damage. Following suitable representations by the army the charge was reduced to 1s. per week per vehicle.

Hitherto livestock sold at the market had been limited to creatures of the four-legged variety, but in August 1915 the committee decided to permit sales of poultry and agreed the following tolls:

turkeys and geese	1d. each
other poultry	½d. each
pigeons	½d. each
any other bird	1d. each
rabbits and ferrets	½d. each

Rabbits and ferrets seem an odd variety of 'poultry', but in strained times all business was welcomed, and to add to this eggs could now be sold at the charge of a halfpenny a dozen.

The new tenants of the refreshment shed, Lambert and Norris, received a terse letter regarding their application for a liquor licence, being told that 'the Committee regret they cannot see their way to make this application'. Drunkenness was a problem on market days since there were seven pubs within striking distance of the market gates, and the corporation – wisely – did not want to be accused of contributing to it.[229] These things apart, the First World War largely passed the Cattle Market by.

Charles Stride emigrated to America in 1912, handing the business over to his sons Fred and Walter (W.O.) Stride.[230]

Exit Hobgen's

Hobgen's were somewhat overshadowed by the expansionist activities of Stride & Son at this time, but in November 1915 they received a reprimand from the committee about the state of their premises and told that 'if something is not done at once the matter will be seriously considered before any further renewal of this lease is made'.[231] They signally failed to respond, and a year later the committee resolved to send another warning to them: 'in view of the bad effect which the dilapidated condition of the buildings has had on the appearance of the Market they will seriously have to consider whether the lease ought to be renewed'. While Hobgens were dithering over surrendering their lease, Walter Stride wasted no time in seeking to have their large shed transferred to him. However, it was not until October 1918 that the matter was finally sorted out; Stride's acquired the lease of Hobgen's double shed, but Hobgen's maintained a presence, taking over some of Stride's small sheds in return.[232] Stride's new premises were soon put to other uses, with the first furniture sale being held there in April 1920, and the committee authorised deadstock sales on non-market days. In April 1922 Hobgen's finally drew stumps and gave up their remaining sheds, leaving the market to Stride's and Wyatt's. Needless to say, Stride's quickly took over the vacated premises.[233]

Wyatt and Son

MESSRS.

WYATT & SON

Auctioneers, Valuers, Surveyors and Estate Agents

59 East St., Chichester

(Established 1826)

Branches at HIGH ST., SELSEY-ON-SEA and 10 WEST ST., HAVANT.

Telephones: CHICHESTER 196. SELSEY 25. HAVANT 11

MARKETS : Chichester alternate Wednesdays. Havant every Tuesday.

Auction Sales of Live and Dead Farming Stock, Timber, Furniture and Household Effects, Stocks-in-Trade and Property of all descriptions conducted in any part of the Country.

Valuations of Tenant-right, Live and Dead Farming Stock, Furniture and Household Effects, Stocks-in-Trade and Property of all descriptions made for Transfer, Probate and other purposes.

Surveys, Reports and Inventories made.
Estates Managed.   Rents Collected

AGENTS to the LEADING INSURANCE COMPANIES

Agents for Farms and Estates to be let or sold, also Residences, Shops and Business Premises, Building Plots and Seaside Bungalows

Head Office : **59 East St., Chichester**

85 *An advertisement placed by Wyatt and Son in the 1933 Kelly's Chichester Directory, which shows that the Cattle Market was but a small part of their overall business.*

The other auction house operating in the Cattle Market, Wyatt and Son, maintained a somewhat low profile through these times, obviously playing second fiddle to Stride & Son even though they had been established much earlier, in 1826. The founder was Edward Wyatt, a farmer from Chidham, who branched out first into agricultural valuation and then auctioneering. He moved the business from Little London to 59 East Street in 1875. By 1882 the business was largely being run by Edward's son Oliver (O.N.) Wyatt, who at the turn of the century took over the former Unitarian chapel in Baffins Lane as an auction room.[234] O.N. Wyatt extended his agricultural interests in 1910 when, as we saw in Chapter Six, he became a director of the Corn Exchange Company, rising to become chairman in 1914, a post he held until 1920.

In the Cattle Market Wyatt & Son specialised in pigs and poultry, and in 1920 began annual sales of pure-bred birds. This was so successful that in 1924 they applied to lease the whole of the poultry shed, but were only granted part of it.[235]

Unlike Stride's, Wyatt's at this time did not seem to be a source of much bother for the corporation, that is until 1925 when they began to flex their muscles and sought to get the rent for their office reduced, and later, in 1926, were successful in getting two rows of pig pens covered in by the corporation, paying £45 a year while they used it but being reminded by the committee that it was not for their use alone.[236]

86 *A sizeable crowd has gathered to witness the noisy departure of the corporation's Leyland fire engine from the new fire station in the corner of the Cattle Market. The crew are resplendent in their brass helmets and ride on the running boards. Stride's large corrugated-iron shed can be seen in the background. Today nothing remains of the fire station, but its position is marked by a section of new wall.*

The new fire station

The corporation maintained a fire brigade that operated out of a small station in Eastgate Square, next to the police station. The original appliances were horse-drawn, but with the move to large motorised fire engines the accommodation became too cramped, and so a site for a new fire station was sought. The site was found in the Cattle Market, and was agreed at a meeting on site, chaired by the mayor, in January 1926.

Walter Stride had been interviewed and agreed to release part of one of his large sheds adjacent to Market Road for conversion into what was described as a 'fire engine house'. Needless to say this involved a great deal of negotiation between the corporation and Stride, who sold the portion required for £95, subject to the corporation providing him with a new dairy shed and more paving. Stride's were also permitted to hold general auctions in the company's large sheds and to create a new doorway through the wall to provide independent access.

The Fire Brigade Committee approved the city surveyor's plans and specifications for the new building, which was added to the west end of the northernmost of Stride's sheds, with part of the brick and flint boundary wall taken down to give access into Market Road. The contract was awarded to Mr Lambert for £591 11s. in August 1926, and the work was completed the following March. The old fire station in Eastgate Square was sold on 25 May 1927 but it is still there. After many years of occupation by W. Goodridge and Co., who sold motorcycles, it is now the Sussex Camera Shop.[237] The new fire station remained in use until 1965, when another one was built at Northgate.

The inter-war years

The motor car began to make its invasive presence felt in Chichester in the late 1920s, and as car ownership increased places were needed to park them. In December 1926 it was agreed to remove three rows of pens close to the weighbridge to create a car park, and three years later a sign was provided to advertise the fact that motorists could now park in the Cattle Market. As steady expansion of the market had been taking place before this, the fact that three rows of pens could be unceremoniously dispensed with seems, on the face of it, a bit strange.

Despite this, Wyatt's managed to secure increased accommodation for their poultry and egg sales and some new traders entered the market, namely D. Rowe & Co. and Allman & Hunt, both agricultural machinery suppliers.

Another reshuffling of the city council in December 1931 saw the affairs of the Cattle Market transferred to a new Highways, Paving, Cattle Market, Lighting, Canal and Fire Brigade Committee, whose diverse title must have made its chairman feel like Pooh-Bah – Lord High Everything Else! In May 1932 the entrance to the market off Eastgate Square was set back to allow for the construction of new public lavatories north of the chapel. Under this scheme the wrought-iron gates were removed and put into storage, and two years later they were gifted to the Parks Committee, who re-erected them at the main entrance to Priory Park – where they remain to this day.[238]

From 1934 the minute clerk reduced the committee's ponderous title to Highways Committee, although its far-reaching powers remained, and in April 1937 it oversaw the demise of the corporation's fleet of horse-drawn vehicles; transport was now entrusted

87 *The main entrance to Priory Park, 2011. The wrought-iron gates started life in 1871 at the Eastgate Square entrance to the Cattle Market but, following redundancy, they were transferred here in 1934.*

to horseless carriages, so the redundant animals and vehicles were sold off and the stable keeper was given notice. The stables were opposite the Cattle Market and still remain in use as a council depot. As the storm clouds of another world war began to gather, a suggestion that the north end of the market be used for roller skating was refused by the committee, as was the city band's request to hold Sunday concerts there.[239] That same year Walter Stride, who had become a city councillor in 1933, was elected Mayor of Chichester.[240]

At war again

On the outbreak of the Second World War the Ministry of Food decided to buy up fatstock in order to control the supply, and in 1941 the Ministry of War Transport set up a portable office in the Cattle Market to direct the lorries being used in the Meat Pool Vehicles Scheme. For the duration only store-stock was being sold on the open market, the ministry acquiring the fatstock at their grading markets held on Mondays. The National Fire Service was given permission to set up a drill tower in November 1942, and the following year the famous mulberry tree was destroyed, not as a result of enemy action but because it had died and was becoming a danger to the public.

The Cattle Market did receive some war damage, however, from the attentions of the United States Air Force. On 11 May 1944 a USAF Liberator bomber, based at Lavenham in Suffolk, got into difficulties over Chichester when an engine caught fire. The crew bailed out and pointed the stricken aircraft out to sea, but it turned around and came back inland, crashing on the Electric Laundry in Velyn Avenue, just the other side of the Cattle Market wall. The crash occurred at 3.55 p.m. and amazingly, considering the time of day and lack of warning, only three lives were lost.[241]

The resulting blast from exploding aircraft fuel travelled across the Cattle Market and caused extensive damage to Stride's sale ring shed, the rebuilding of which began later that month. In 1945 part of the wall alongside the Whyke Lane twitten, which had no doubt been weakened by the blast, had to be shored up pending the addition of new brick buttresses.

The annual rental income listed in the minutes for 14 February 1945 gives an idea of the relative sizes of the two tenant operations: Stride & Son, in their dominant position, contributed 68 per cent of the income against Wyatt's 12 per cent, the remaining 20 per cent being made up of rental of spare land and advertising space.

1949 – the top of the slippery slope

The year 1949 was to prove pivotal in the fortunes of the Cattle Market, as it marked the start of a decline that was to lead to its demise some 40 years later. In January a new auctioneer applied to enter the ring, namely Whitehead & Whitehead. This firm of estate agents and auctioneers had been established in 1899 and opened an office in Chichester at 18 South Street. In their application they requested the building of a new sale ring and standings for their proposed sales of cattle, thereby challenging the duopoly of Messrs Stride and Wyatt. This was to prove a tough nut for the corporation to crack, and as a first move the Market Sub-committee sought the views of the Ministry of Agriculture, Fisheries and Food on the number of auctioneers who ought to be allowed to operate in the market. Sadly their response – if any – is not recorded.

In Chapter Four (see p.52) we encountered the Provisional Order that the corporation obtained in 1949 to revise the provisions of both the Market House Act of 1807 and the Cattle Market Act of 1868. This Order enabled the corporation to change the way the business of the two markets could be conducted and allowed a complete revision of the cattle market tolls. This they did, giving a 100 per cent increase under most headings, and adding tolls for the sale of motor vehicles and tractors which, not surprisingly, had not been provided for in the 1868 Act.[242]

February 1949 saw the publication of Thomas Sharp's infamous report 'Georgian Chichester – A plan for the preservation and improvement of Chichester'. Sharp had been commissioned by the corporation in 1947 to produce a report making recommendations about the future of the city. In his report Sharp's ideas on both 'preservation' and 'improvement' were somewhat wide of the meanings we attach to those words today. He recommended the demolition of virtually everything immediately outside the bounds of the Roman city and the building of a ring road hugging its walls. It was this report that led to the controversial destruction of the east side of Somerstown in 1964. Sharp's report also had implications – and unhappy prognoses – for the Cattle Market, as this extract shows:

> [The Cattle Market] is well situated, and may be allowed to remain here. But it will be necessary to curtail its present size. The new ring road cannot be taken into Eastgate Square. It must be swung eastwards to a new square to be developed between the Hornet and St Pancras: and this will involve its being run across the northern part of the Market. This, however, need not interfere unduly with the Market's continuance; for, though it is still a busy and important affair, the number of cattle passing through it has recently declined somewhat because of new methods of marketing – and it is not unlikely, indeed, that the whole market may become redundant in twenty or thirty years' time ... a new COVERED MARKET would be well sited adjoining the Cattle Market on the east.[243]

When the report was published it naturally gave rise to many uncertainties; Wyatt and Son saw that their poultry shed would have to be demolished to make way for the new road, and Mr Stride queried whether it was worth his while investing £1,500 to provide the separate accommodation needed for him to sell tuberculin-tested (TT) cattle.

The city surveyor was ordered to prepare a 'comprehensive report' on the state and scope of the market.[244] Indeed, so concerned were the corporation about the future direction of their markets that they separated them from the affairs of highways and established a new body called the Special (Cattle Market) Committee, which met for the first time on 27 April 1949. Their first task was to consider proposals being put forward by Stride & Son, Wyatt & Son and the would-be new entrant Whitehead & Whitehead. They made three resolutions: firstly to invite the local branches of the Young Farmers Club and the National Farmers Union (NFU) along with the West Sussex County Agricultural Committee to join a conference on how to improve the Cattle Market, secondly to invite the three firms of auctioneers to the next committee meeting, and lastly to arrange visits to the markets at Exeter and Guildford to see how they managed their business.

The city surveyor produced two sets of plans for a reordering of the market that September, the first providing an interim arrangement with a new poultry shed, restaurant and corn market, and the second the 'ultimate arrangement', removing the city surveyor's depot and accommodating Sharp's ring road. The latter scheme was the one approved by the committee. One outcome of the jollies to Exeter and Guildford was that a full-time market superintendent was employed in November, in the person of Mr A.N. Harrison, on a salary of between £450 and 495 a year plus removal expenses.[245]

Thomas Sharp had hinted at the declining state of the Cattle Market and this, unfortunately, was borne out by the year-end accounts presented on 31 March 1949, which showed expenditure of £2,304 9s. 9d. against a total income of only £1,484 0s. 11d. – the balance having to be made up from the corporation's general fund.[246]

The year 1949 ended with the death of Walter Stride, whose memorial service on 21 December saw the cathedral packed with his colleagues from the agricultural and civic worlds.[247]

88 *Walter Stride and his wife Gwen at an unidentified agricultural event.*

Into the 1950s

J.E. and J.P. Whitehead attended the February 1950 meeting of the special committee to plead their case for entering the Cattle Market in competition with the two resident auctioneers, prompting a subsequent meeting with Wyatt's and Stride's to seek their views. These consultations formed the corporation's view that competitive selling by auction could not be entertained; instead Stride's and Wyatt's were offered new five-year leases to conduct sales that did not compete with each other. Not easily deterred, Whitehead & Whitehead applied again in February 1951, only to be told that their request could not be considered 'for the time being owing to restrictions of space'.

An order to allow the market to be held weekly instead of fortnightly was granted in 1952, and that same year a new enclosed sale ring and shed for TT cattle, designed by the city surveyor, was erected.[248]

Most of Thomas Sharp's ideas, including the new road across the Cattle Market, were (mercifully) not to be implemented, but a scheme for the widening of Market Road along its eastern side was drawn up in 1953. This involved demolition of the west wall of the Cattle Market and its reconstruction further east, the provision of a new main entrance and the re-siting of affected buildings within the market – all at the expense of West Sussex County Council. Work commenced in August 1954 and was largely complete by the following November.[249]

The end of wartime austerity came officially in 1954 when the Ministry of Food freed up the purchase of fatstock and closed their weekly grading markets, but this good news was offset by the NFU proposing that both the resident auctioneers should now sell the full range of livestock in order to give farmers an element of choice. Competition, the NFU pointed out, was taking place at other markets. Stride's and Wyatt's were unhappy with this rocking of the boat and wrote to the committee to say they could not reach an agreement with the NFU on such a change. That did it: nothing more was heard about the proposal, so the cosy, restrictive practices continued.

Among the new facilities provided in 1954 was an office for the market superintendent built next to the re-sited entrance. For this the city surveyor tabled a design for a circular building which unfortunately failed to impress the committee, who ordered him to come back with a design for a square one. The diligent surveyor duly produced the alternative design and was ordered to seek tenders for both; in the event the circular building proved the cheaper and so was built. It still stands today, bearing the legend 'Market Office', and was the only Cattle Market building to survive the wholesale demolition in 1990.

After a disagreement about suitable facilities the Ministry of Food approved Chichester Cattle market as a liveweight certification centre for

89 *Inside the new sale ring during a sale of attested cattle in 1957. It was totally enclosed from the elements and brought unheard-of comforts for auctioneers and bidders alike. Some bidders lean on the rails while others resort to the relative luxury of the tiered benches.*

90 *The exterior of the 1952 sale ring when it was awaiting demolition in 1990.*

cattle and pigs on 21 June 1954, but this status was only granted for six months at a time, and was constantly threatened with withdrawal owing to the inadequacy of facilities.

John Willis joined Wyatt and Son as an auctioneer in 1950 but left in 1953, only to return in 1955 as a partner in Stride & Son, by which time Pat Stride, Walter's son, was running the family business. After holding his first cattle sale in 1955 John Willis described the state of the market as 'desperate', as so few beasts were being put up for sale. He saw that closure of the market was becoming a real threat, and began to travel out to local farms to drum up business.[250] He always cut a dash in the sale ring with his selection of hats.

Further perceived inadequacies, this time in matters of hygiene, led to the replacement of the refreshment shed by a new timber refreshment room

91 *The refreshment room built in 1958 and sited next to Market Road. It was known to its frequenters as the Chicken Shed. The former Baptist chapel, now Eastgate Hall, is seen in the right background.*

in 1958. This was built at the north end of the market alongside Market Road, and provided facilities for the serving of teas and snacks together with a bar, run by Brickwood's of Portsmouth, to cater for the needs of those farmers who required something a bit stronger. The room, known by its customers as the Chicken Shed, was licensed for public entertainments and made available for hire on non-market days, the Sunshine Club and the city band being among its first users.[251]

The town clerk, dissatisfied with the income from the market, sought counsel's advice in December 1958 on the rental value of the buildings and the matter of competitive auctioneering, thus reopening a can of worms. Following this the corporation resolved to terminate the existing leases in September 1959 under Clause 25 of the Landlord and Tenant Act (1954) and to renegotiate the same with Stride's and Wyatt's. While Wyatt's offer of £1,250 a year was accepted, that of Stride's, at £1,500, was not, and this sparked a battle that made previous struggles pale into insignificance. The town clerk advised Stride's solicitors that they were looking at not less than £1,850 a year, but Pat Stride stuck to his guns and took the matter to the High Court. The hearing took place on 22 January 1960 and the court found in favour of Stride, that £1,500 was a fair rent. To add insult to their injury, the corporation was ordered to pay Stride's legal costs.[252]

Enter the traders' market

The idea of including a weekly traders' market was floated by the Chichester Trades Council in 1947, as was reported in the October edition of the *Chichester Review*, where a spokesman reported that they had met the town clerk and the 'cost would be negligible compared to the benefit the citizens would get and the ultimate income to the council'. The committee had, in fact, supported the idea and agreed to provide the stalls for a market that should be held on Fridays and Saturdays. The city surveyor was sent away to prepare plans for building 10 lean-to stalls, and four sectional buildings to act as offices, all sited along the Whyke Lane wall. In the event only the offices were built, in September 1948, but they proved so popular that two more were added the following month.[253] The 1949 Provisional Order empowered the corporation to set up such a traders' market in the Cattle

Market but, as we saw in Chapter Four, this proposal was not popular with Chichester's shopkeepers, who feared the flooding of the market by 'cheapjack' goods. The idea then went off the boil – but did not go away.

It was not until July 1959 that approval was finally given for the purchase of 20 portable stalls for market traders, and the erection of a building to provide washing facilities. The terms for trading included that not more than three traders could sell goods of the same kind, the sale of fresh meat, fish and shellfish was not permitted and only wrapped groceries (as received from the manufacturers) could be sold. The market would trade on Fridays and Saturdays between the hours of 10 a.m. and 4 p.m.

The traders' market opened on 3 June 1960, but the stall-holders soon proved a troublesome lot who petitioned for some basic protection against the elements. When the latter was not provided they withheld their rents and petitioned to have the Friday market moved to Wednesday in order to coincide with the cattle market – they even offered to pay an extra £4 10s. to compensate for the car-parking fees that would be lost as a result of their stalls being in position. The two livestock market tenants objected to the Wednesday traders' market and so initially it was not permitted, but following further representations the corporation relented and agreed to Wednesday trading commencing on 16 November 1960, in addition to Fridays and Saturdays. A further change was to permit the selling of goods by 'pitching' (i.e. informal auction) instead of fixed price retailing.

Unfortunately the three-day traders' market did not prove as lucrative as hoped, so the traders invoked the National Market Traders' Federation, who suggested to the corporation that the market be held on Wednesdays only, with reduced rents and increased publicity so as to attract more traders and the public. The Markets Committee agreed to this and so the market became a Wednesdays-only affair with rents reduced to 12s. 6d. a week.

One non-market use of the site that was granted each year was for the forming of the annual Gala Day carnival procession that took place on the first Saturday of July. Local organisations assembled their floats on lorries loaned by local businesses, and the procession, led by a military band, wound its way around the city.[254]

92 *Some of the offices in the north-east corner of the Cattle Market. These sectional buildings were put up in 1948.*

The 1960s – a decade of challenges

Although the beast market had been gone from the streets some 90 years by the start of the 1960s, farm animals were still a feature of the street scene on Wednesdays when they were driven from the station or local farms. One drover of particular note was Ted Gobey, a man with only one arm who was invariably the worse for drink. He also possessed a rich vocabulary of swear words, which delighted and educated hundreds of Chichester schoolboys – your author included. On Gala Day he would enter the arena and march up and down beside the band (often the Royal Marines) hurling abuse, until the strong arm of Sussex Police removed him. As the 1960s wore on, road transport replaced rail for livestock, and so the animals, and their colourful drovers, disappeared from the streets of Chichester.

At this time Wyatt and Son expanded their monthly general auctions of small items to include bicycles, garden machinery, furniture and vehicles, which breathed a bit of new life into the ailing market site, but not enough to revive its fortunes.[255]

With some justification the 1960s are regarded as the most philistine period in modern history as far as town planning is concerned, a decade in which much of our architectural heritage was destroyed in the name of progress. As it happened, the needless destruction of the east side of Somerstown apart, Chichester escaped relatively lightly, but developers were casting their greedy eyes over the Cattle Market and the prime site it occupied.

It was at the special Market Committee's meeting on 14 December 1964 that the question of moving the Cattle Market to a new site first surfaced, but consideration of it was deferred until the highway proposals for the city had been finalised. These proposals included a ring road, to be created by widening the existing highways around three of the quadrants and completed by cutting a new link across Westgate Fields from Westgate to Southgate. Market Road would form part of this ring road. In the

93 *Cattle being driven through Eastgate Square in 1966, having come from a farm to the east of the city. In the background is St Pancras Church and the former Gaumont cinema, which had closed six years earlier and was about to be converted into Chichester's first public swimming pool.*

94 *An extract from the 1964 Ordnance Survey (1:2500 scale) showing the changes brought about in the previous decade. The new entrance from Market Road can be seen opposite the Corporation Yard, with the circular market office next to it. To the north of the entrance can be seen the refreshment room adjacent to the Baptist chapel. The fire station is still in the south-west corner but it was to close the following year. In the south-east corner is the new sale ring and adjoining cattle shed. To the north of the sale ring it can be seen that many pens have been removed to provide car parking, an indication of the declining fortunes of the market.*

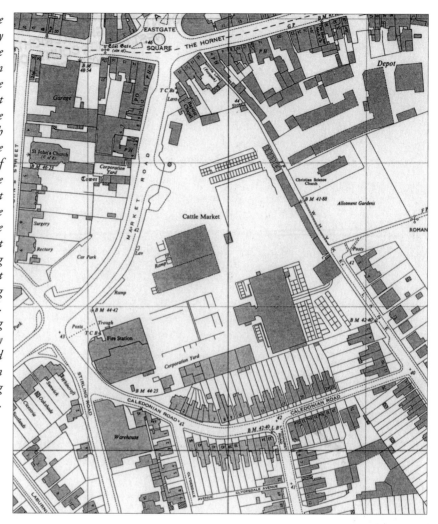

meantime the fire brigade moved to shiny new premises at Northgate in 1965, and what had now become the 'old' fire station was used for car auctions from February 1966.[256]

The special committee's reign came to an end in April 1966 when the business of the markets was taken over by a new body, ponderously entitled the Markets, Cemetery, Parks and Allotments Committee, a title that was pragmatically shortened to Parks Committee at its first meeting on 6 June 1966.

The matter of the move to another site came to the new committee's attention in December 1968, when it was reported that the town clerk and city surveyor had met the markets officer of the Ministry of Agriculture, Fisheries and Food (MAFF), who favoured a proposed move of the Cattle Market to a new out-of-town location. The following July the district valuer agreed to pay £145,000 for the disused Portfield Tip, an area of 31.45 acres, of which 6.3 acres would be used to create a new cattle market and the remainder for housing. Progress with this stalled, for in January 1969 a sub-committee, formed of Aldermen Newell and Pope and chaired by the mayor, Tomas Siggs, was charged with examining the need for a cattle market in the Chichester area. In the meantime the tenants were permitted to hold over the terms of their expired leases. Things really were not looking good. The prognosis worsened in September when the Public Health and Housing Committee opined that the council would not be interested in buying Portfield Tip at the price now demanded by the vendor. The sub-committee concurred with this and refused a request by the local branch of the NFU for a council representative to address their next meeting on the future of the Cattle Market.

The sub-committee finally reported their findings – which had involved much consultation – in April 1970. There was some support for the retention of a market in Chichester, 'but this is very limited and cannot justify the continued operation of a market within the city'. The existing lessees wanted to see the Cattle Market adapted for the next 10 years but the sub-committee felt that this was unsatisfactory and would frustrate the planned development. It was thought that securing the land at Portfield would involve 'very substantial expenditure' but this was not seen as ruling out the possibility of another site in the rural area. Stride & Son had identified proposals for segregating accredited cattle from others, but they had to decide whether the proposals were viable 'for the limited life of the market'.[257] From this we can infer that a developer was in tow, but he was not identified. Indecision on the Cattle Market's future reigned supreme for over a year until the meeting of 21 June 1971, when the many representations that had been made to retain the Cattle Market were considered, along with the idea of building a multi-storey car park over the site. The result was – still no decision! Instead the committee resolved to tell the lessees that it would not be possible both to redevelop the site and retain the cattle market at the same time (apart from the traders' stalls) and that 'the life of the market could extend well beyond 1974, until possibly 1978'. They also resolved to close the refreshment room and use it as a mess room for council workers, albeit still being available for letting in the evenings. They opined that the loss of this facility would not be of concern to the general public and refreshments would henceforth be provided from a van. As the writing seemed to be on the proverbial wall it was decided to terminate the council's membership of the National Association of British Market Authorities.

The NFU continued to campaign for retention of the market, and so in June 1972 it was agreed to set up a joint working party consisting of

95 *John Willis of Stride & Son conducting a cattle auction, summer 1970. As always he is sporting a hat – this time a seasonal straw panama.*

representatives from the NFU, the council and the lessees. However, one has to wonder whether the councillors' hearts were really in it; it was by then known that the reorganisation of local government being ushered in by the Heath government would do away with Chichester City Council as a corporation, and that it would thus be left to a new administration to take the closure and redevelopment – or otherwise – of the Cattle Market forward.

The Parks Committee's final meeting took place on 18 February 1974, and their last business was that of granting a pedestrian right of way across the market site to the purchaser of 19 Caledonian Road, the former tied house of the market superintendent that had just been sold. If there was any sadness expressed about the imminent demise of Chichester City Council, or hopes for what was to come, it was not recorded. Instead the last words in the minute book are a vote of thanks to the chairman, Cllr Smith, for the way he had conducted the committee's business and his thanking of the committee for their support. After 103 years the old order at Chichester Cattle Market under Chichester City Council had ended, and a new era was about to begin under the control of the fledgling Chichester District Council.

The new broom

Chichester District Council, which assumed most of the functions of Chichester City Council, came into power in April 1974, and the affairs of the Cattle Market were entrusted to the Public Services Committee, which quickly set up a sub-committee to deal with day-to-day issues. The delicate matter of the future of the market seems to have been temporarily swept under the carpet by the new broom, for it was not until February 1975 that meetings were held with Messrs Stride and Wyatt. A verbal report of the meeting was given at the committee meeting of 26 March, but no details thereof were recorded in the minutes.[258] Over a year later the council appointed Henry Smith & Son of Horsham to act on their behalf in negotiating revised leases with Stride's and Wyatt's, but the report given to the committee meeting of 10 October 1976 was to the effect that the negotiations had failed. The council's chief executive drew attention to the new Chichester Corridor Plan, and the fact that it would be necessary to look again at the idea of moving the Cattle Market to Portfield and reappraise the consequent use of the existing site, especially as West Sussex County Council had abandoned their road scheme that would have cut across it. Furthermore the district council's works department were to vacate the Cattle Market for a new site at Westhampnett in November, freeing up more space. As such it was resolved to take no further action on the leases, and to terminate Henry Smith's appointment as agent.

One important driver in the council's thinking was capitalising on the shrinking state of the market by increased use of the site for car parking. In March 1977 they reached agreement with Wyatt and Son to surrender the part of their land used for the sale of pigs and sheep, retaining only that for poultry and livestock. The engineer and surveyor then produced a £3,800 scheme for moving the wash-down facility and resurfacing the former Wyatt area, on completion of which two-thirds of the Cattle Market would be available for car parking purposes. A definite pattern was emerging. Part of the old works buildings were demolished in 1977, creating 10 further car parking spaces and also allowing the now redundant western part of the site to be offered to the housing department. The engineer and surveyor tabled new plans, which, with a relocation of the traders' market into the now-redundant pig shed, would give a total of 380 car parking spaces.[259]

At this critical time Stride & Son took on a new member of staff, Derek Bowerman, who was immediately urged by Pat Stride to try auctioning cattle. At this he proved most adept, and so he joined John Willis on the rostrum; from then on the two of them conducted the whole day's livestock sales. Auctioning of cattle was not without its excitements, and Derek Bowerman recalls one day when a seemingly placid lean cow, having passed through the weighbridge and entered the ring, suddenly took it into her head to escape via the narrow pedestrian entrance. Derek watched in horror as, in the course of her charge, she became firmly wedged by her hip bones in the bars and could not move. Initial thoughts were to call the fire brigade to cut out the bars, but in the end several burly farmers came to the rescue and managed to lift her up clear of the bars and put her back into the ring. Mercifully they were not treated to an unwelcome shower of ordure in the process! On another occasion some cattle were brought up from Devon by train for sale. At the end of a two-day journey they were, understandably, frustrated, and so they were driven on a few laps of the cattle market to calm them down. Unfortunately, however, despite the long distances some animals were being brought, the numbers sold were still declining as arable farming took over from husbandry again.[260]

The first action of the district council with respect to the traders' market was to double the stall rents from £1.25 to £2.50 per day in July 1974. At this time the traders' market was still held in the open, but in February 1978 the newer part of the now-redundant pig shed was repaired and made available for market traders, who could now operate under cover. The rents were increased again, the new rates being £5 per day for a covered site and £4 for one in the open – but at least the traders' market was still growing.

Unfortunately the traders were not too enamoured with their new facilities, and in March 1979 they presented the council with a petition expressing their dissatisfaction. This precipitated a meeting with the engineer and surveyor, who found that while two thirds of the traders accepted the new layout they wanted the area inside the shed to be resurfaced and permission to be granted for butchers and fishmongers to trade. Both requests were granted.[261] Less fortunate, however, were Golden Bargain Markets, who applied to the district council in August 1981 to hold Sunday markets. Strong objections were lodged by the Chamber of Commerce, 44 market traders, 183 residents and the rector of St Pancras and St John. Although the city council were in favour of a Sunday market the district council Public Services Committee voted unanimously to refuse it. The tradition of eschewing Sunday trading in a cathedral city remained unshaken.

The traders' market continued to grow, and a new layout was approved by the committee in January 1982 that would provide a total of 96 stalls but require £600 to be invested in repairs to the pig shed structure. To pay for the improvements the rents were increased yet again, to £10 per day under cover and £8 outside. The Wednesday trader's market was now thriving, with virtually everything being available there, and it was rapidly eclipsing the cattle market for public attention. On 2 April 1983 the Saturday market was reintroduced and proved an instant success. Then, in the true spirit of Thatcherism, the management of the trader's market was privatised.[262]

96 *A sheep sale conducted by Derek Bowerman of Stride & Son assisted by Imogen Stuart, the auctioneer's clerk, May 1990. Note the characteristically stony expressions of the customers, which give nothing away.*

Decline and fall

January 1982 heralded the beginning of the end of livestock marketing, when the two auctioneers applied to have their leases renewed. In debating this the committee remained in favour of retaining the livestock market on the current site, but the director of development services pointed out that the Chichester and Downland Plan provided for its relocation at Tangmere, with only the traders' market remaining. It was finally agreed to grant leases of two and a half years instead of three, as the site was likely to be repossessed.

The following year the wall adjacent to Market Road began to show signs of distress, and a debate raged over whether the cost of rebuilding could be justified in the light of the uncertainty; that perhaps a reduction in height should be made instead. In 1984 the lowering of the wall went ahead, opening up a new vista of the market site from Market Road.

Car parking continued to exercise the district council's mind at this time, and a study was commissioned from consultants who recommended that, owing to the increasing demand, the parking implications of any new uses for the Cattle Market be taken into account. They went on to suggest that a multi-storey car park could be built over the site.[263]

The Chichester Society had been formed in 1974 as a campaigning group for Chichester's inhabitants, and in 1986 they took up the challenge of retaining the Cattle Market. Throughout June and July they manned a stall at the Wednesday market, collecting some 5,000 signatures in favour of keeping both the livestock and traders' markets on the Eastgate site. They went on to publish a report setting out their case. Its introduction ran:

> Years of planning blight have left Chichester's Cattle Market site in its present rundown condition. Nevertheless, both the cattle and stall markets form an essential part of the city's character, and the many thousands of people who use them strongly wish them to be retained and improved on the present site. Months of careful study have shown us how important it is that any reorganisation should be for the benefit of the people of Chichester and its visitors, not for achieving the maximum commercial return from a piece of real estate, nor to accommodate any unwanted new roads. This booklet examines the principal issues involved and provides some positive suggestions for the future.[264]

This introduction set out the tenor of the campaign, and the report, peppered with quotations from users, set out the case for retention and development of the market. Both Stride's and Wyatt's had contributed to the text with views on how, with a complete reorganisation of the site and no reduction in its area, the businesses of the two markets could be consolidated and built upon. The Chichester Society's conclusion was:

In our opinion, these are the essential considerations, but equally we must stress that this large site provides a rare opportunity to develop a host of other imaginative schemes which could not only enhance the life of the city but attract important extra revenue to help relieve the burden of rates.

97   *The Saturday Market, Chichester. One of several charming drawings by David Goodman, the founder of the Chichester Society, which illustrated their campaigning report on the retention of the Cattle Market.*

Although the report claimed to have the support of some councillors the seed seemed to have fallen upon stony ground, at least as far as the livestock market was concerned.

On the night of 16 October 1987 the south of England was hit by a hurricane that caused widespread damage throughout the Chichester area. The Cattle Market was not spared, and one mature tree was uprooted, bringing down 20yds of the boundary wall next to the Whyke Lane twitten. Many Whyke Lane residents wrote to the council fearing that, owing to the uncertainty about the future of the market, repairs would not be made. This damage was repaired, but the following year, when the engineer and

98   *Life goes on regardless: Wyatt's annual sale of turkeys in the deadstock shed on 22 December 1988.*

surveyor identified £10,000-worth of repairs to the concrete wash-down area, he was ordered to spend only £3,000 'in view of possible redevelopment'.

A Market Redevelopment Sub-committee was set up in 1988, and this instructed the director of development services to prepare a brief for the redevelopment of the Cattle Market site. In April 1989, after receiving reports from the sub-committee, the full council resolved to reduce the size of the livestock market, clear the remainder of the site and resurface it for car parking.[265]

The following June another committee was set up, the Eastgate Development Special Committee, which had a wider brief to look at the future of the area around Eastgate Square. They met Derek Bowerman of Stride & Son to discuss a rationalisation of the livestock market. His view was that a rationalised market could work, but that relocation to another site was not an option. Councillor Louise Bassett, who chaired this committee, told its members that if Stride's wished to continue trading in the Cattle Market they should contribute to the costs of reordering it. Derek Bowerman submitted a proposed layout and business plan for the *de minimis* scheme, by which time the council had received an interim report from its consultant, Rural Planning Services Ltd, who had looked at the options for the livestock market. Citing the reduction in throughput and the poor state of the buildings, they felt that relocation was the only option that would keep it alive – to do nothing would effectively close it.

The council's mind now seemed to have been made up, for it was decided in September 1989 to terminate all leases but Stride's in March 1990, including that of Prudential Property Services, who had taken over Wyatt's business the previous year.[266] On 6 March 1990, at a full meeting of Chichester District Council, a vote was taken on the motion 'that the land at present leased to Messrs Stride for the purposes of the livestock market be used for the Council's own purposes, namely car parking, and that the necessary planning application be submitted'. This was carried by 29 votes to twelve. The die had been cast and the livestock market was doomed.[267]

Stride & Son was now the sole trader in the Cattle Market, and had taken on Prudential's sheep sales, but their tenancy was due to expire on 20 September 1990. It was negotiated that the site was to be vacated by 30 September, after which time Messrs Tarmac, who were already converting the Cattle Market into a car park, would have their contract extended to complete the job. It was agreed that 15 of the cast-iron posts and their attendant rails from the former pens would be retained for use on the new section of the South Wall near Cawley Priory, which was about to be opened to the public.*

---

* In fact 23 posts were used on the Walls Walk near Cawley Priory, where they can be seen on the ramps up to the wall.

In the event matters were delayed by a month; the last ever livestock market was to be held on 24 October 1990, but the weekly traders' markets would continue.[268]

The last day of Chichester Cattle Market, Wednesday 24 October 1990

The last day of livestock trading in Chichester, and the demise of Chichester Cattle Market, was marked with due ceremony and much reflection. Under the headline 'Final livestock sale ends great tradition', the *Chichester Observer* of 25 October 1990 reported that the market bell was rung to mark the final death knell and quoted the Chichester Society chairman, David Goodman, as saying that in his opinion the reasons given for the closure had been inadequate. Inside a further full-page report on the day's proceedings was given accompanied by seven

99 *A chalked notice on a message board dated 24 October 1990 says it all. The board was carefully taken down at the end of the day and can now be seen in Chichester District Museum.*

100 *John Willis, wearing a black Stetson hat, conducting the last cattle sale on 24 October 1990. The chalked inscription on the makeshift rostrum heralds the imminent arrival of the car park, while a small boy peers pensively through the rails. One wonders whether he remembers this momentous day.*

STRIDE & SON
SURVEYORS & VALUERS
AUCTIONEERS, HOUSE & ESTATE AGENTS
CENTENARY YEAR 1890-1990

John D. Willis, F.R.I.C.S, F.C.A.A.V.
Derek J. Bowerman, B.Sc.(Econ.), F.R.I.C.S.
Mark A. Hewitt, F.R.I.C.S. (Furniture Saleroom)
Nicholas J. Stride, F.S.V.A. (Property)

*Southdean House,
St. John's Street,
Chichester.*
PO19 1XQ

Telephone
CHICHESTER (0243) 780626 – 3 lines
780207 (Furniture Saleroom)
Fax (0243) 786713

CHICHESTER LIVESTOCK MARKET CLOSURE
24th October, 1990.

LAST CALF – Limousin Bull –   Sold by Barnham Court Farms
                                Purchaser – C. Pitman of Eastergate

        Auctioneer – Mark Hewitt

LAST SHEEP – Pen of lambs –   Sold by J. Dewey of Bosham
                                Purchaser – J.Harris (Farms) Ltd., Fontley

        Auctioneer – Derek Bowerman

LAST PIGS – Pen of porkers –   Sold by M. Bradbury of Hambrook
                                Purchaser – J. Harris (Farms) Ltd., Fontley

        Auctioneer – Henry Adams

LAST FAT CATTLE – Hereford Cross Heifer
                                Sold by J. Seller of Arundel
                                Purchaser – A.M.Marriott & Son, Arundel

        Auctioneer – John Willis

LAST STORE CATTLE – Charolais steers
                                Sold by C. Green of Hambrook
                                Purchaser – A.M. Harriott & Son, Arundel

        Auctioneer John Willis

LAST BARREN COW, – Friesian   Sold by E.R. Cutler of Southwick (Hants.)
AND LAST BEAST TO BE SOLD   Purchaser – J. Harris (Farms) Ltd., Fontley

        Auctioneer Derek Bowerman

        Auctioneers Clerks: Norman Mills
                            Mrs. Imogen Stewart

        DE MORTUIS NIL NISI BONUM

101   *A typed record of the auctioneers and purchasers at the last sales on 24 October 1990.*

photographs; it was noted that the nearest livestock market was now in Guildford, as two others in Sussex, Haywards Heath and Pulborough, had also closed down.

The last ever sales were conducted by Stride's three auctioneers, Mark Hewitt, Derek Bowerman and John Willis, along with Henry Adams, who had been an auctioneer with Wyatt and Son. Henry Adams later took over the former Wyatt business from Prudential Property Services, and it now trades under his name.

Near the sale ring a Latin inscription had been posted, 'Quam parva sapientia Noviomagus regitur' ('With what little wisdom Chichester is governed'), and at the end of the sales a coffin, bearing the words 'Chichester Market Died October 1990 R.I.P.'

and containing a jeroboam of champagne was brought in. After consumption of the contents of the jeroboam, the coffin and John Willis's hat were presented to Chichester District Museum.

With that, 119 years of Chichester Cattle Market had come to an end, and the bulldozers moved in with indecent haste to flatten the remaining buildings in order that the conversion of the entire site into a car park might be completed.

102   Requiescat in pace. *The coffin symbolising the death of Chichester Cattle Market on 24 October 1990.*

NINE

Postlude: In a Fair Ground

FAIR [of *feyer*, Teut, *foire*, F, both from *feriae*, L, Holidays on which Fairs are usually kept; or of *Forum* L, a Market] an annual and general market for the City, Town &c.

N. Bailey, An Universal Etymological English Dictionary,
London, 1782

As well as the regular weekly markets already considered, Chichester has, since medieval times, held a number of annual fairs. As Bailey's 1782 definition suggests, fairs were general, rather than specific-commodity, markets, but they also came with other attractions and entertainments, not all of which were necessarily of a wholesome sort. They were, in fact, quite different from a normal market in offering something of a day out in holiday mood, and a particular feature was horse-trading – in the literal sense.

The Crown often granted such fairs to local dignitaries, giving them absolute jurisdiction over the proceedings and the benefit of the dues and tolls. The owners were sometimes empowered under the charters to hold 'pie-powder courts', impromptu courts set up to administer speedy justice for both buyers and sellers and mete out redress in the case of (frequent) disorder. It is said that this picturesque term comes from the fact that justice could be had as soon as the dust could fall from the feet of a transgressor or, more etymologically, from the French *pied pouldreaux* – peddlers or petty chapmen who resort to fairs.[269]

There were five ancient fairs held in Chichester, and by the mid-18th century their names and dates were St George's Fair (23 April), Whit Monday Fair (moveable feast), St James's Fair (25 July), Michaelmas Fair (10 October, adhering to the 'old style' date of the feast) and Sloe Fair (19 October).[270] These fairs are not terribly well documented and there is an unfortunate degree of uncertainty about both the venues for some of them and the dates they ceased to exist, since contemporary sources do not always agree. By 1889, according to a Royal Commission on market rights held that year, there were apparently still five fairs being held in Chichester. The dates reported were 4 May, Whit Monday, 5 August, 10 October and 20 October.[271] The fairs are not named but one can see that the dates of some of them had changed, with St George's Fair drifting into May, St James's into August and Sloe Fair to the now-customary date of 20 October.

St George's Fair

St George's Fair was granted by King Henry VII to the Mayor of Chichester by a charter dated 14 May 1500. The fair could be held on 23 April and the two days following, with a pie-powder court to maintain justice.[272] This right was renewed in the two charters granted to the city by King James II in 1685 and 1687.[273]

The original venue for this fair is unclear. Richard Dally in his *Chichester Guide* of 1831 gives it, rather vaguely, as being 'a field in the east suburbs' (as he does for all except Sloe Fair), which may refer to the Michaelmas field in St Pancras. However, by the early 19th century it was being held in the streets.[274] William Hoare and his quaint memoirs of early 19th-century Chichester we have already encountered in Chapter Three; here he gives a flavour of the street fairs:

> for many years there were two fairs held in the centre of the city, one on the fourth May [*sic*] and the other on Whit Monday. Well, these fairs were kept one part in East Street, one in North Street and I have seen the stalls even in South Street on the west side of the cross. They used to play nine pins and throw at snuff boxes, and there was what was called a roundabout pushed by boys, that was always on the East Front of the Cross.[275]

Hoare is describing both the St George's and Whit Monday fairs, and makes no mention of any animal trading taking place: indeed, had St George's Fair fallen on a Wednesday – which it must have done from time to time – there would have been an awkward clash with the regular beast market.

Another memoir, this time of the mid-19th century, was penned by George Tippen in 1925 when he was 88. He recalls only four fairs at that time: Michaelmas, Sloe and 'two Confectionary and Toy Fairs, one held in East Street from St Martin's Corner to the Cross, the other to the Fish Market in North Street'. He goes on to say that 'three of these have been abolished some years leaving only Sloe Fair'.[276]

St George's Fair was abolished in 1873 by an Order from the Secretary of State for the Home Department using the powers of the Fairs Act of 1871. In a draft notice about the proposed abolition the fair is described as being 'held in the Streets of the Said City on the fourth of May'. In the public notices issued in July 1873 it was stated that a representation had been made (on the previous 28 April) by justices acting for the city of Chichester, to the effect that 'it would be for the convenience and advantage of the public that such fairs should be abolished'. Objectors were invited to respond, but had little time to do so. Abolition duly took place on and from the date of the Order, 13 August 1873, so the last ever St George's Fair was that held the previous 4 May.[277]

Whit Monday Fair

Whit Monday is, of course, a movable feast dictated by the timing of Easter and has long been a holiday. The fair held on this date does not seem to have been granted by any charter, but the corporation had ownership of it in the 19th century.[278] Once again Dally gives the location as being a field in the eastern suburbs (possibly the Michaelmas Fair Field), but in the 19th century it too was being held in the streets as Hoare describes above. This fair was abolished by the same Order that did away with St George's Fair; the last Whit Monday Fair was thus held in May 1873.[279]

St James's Fair

The fair held on the feast of St James (25 July) was claimed by Edward I in 1289 when he commanded the sheriff to proclaim it in his name rather than that of Richard Fitzalan, 11th Earl of Arundel, who previously owned it. The fair was held in a field near the Hospital of St James in St Pancras.[280]

William Hoare provides a recollection of what he terms 'St Pancras Fair

THE FAIRS ACT, 1871.

CHICHESTER FAIRS.

WHEREAS, a representation has been duly made to me, as Secretary of State for the Home Department, by the Justices acting in and for the City of Chichester, that Fairs have been annually held on the 4th day of May and on Whit-Monday, in the said City, and that it would be for the convenience and advantage of the public that the said Fairs should be abolished.

And whereas, notice of the said representation and of the time when I should take the same into consideration has been duly published, in pursuance of "The Fairs Act, 1871;" and whereas, on such representation and consideration it appears to me that it would be for the convenience and advantage of the public that the said Fairs should be abolished; and whereas, the Town Council of Chichester, as lords or owners of the said Fairs, and the tolls thereof, have consented in writing that the said Fairs should be abolished.

Now, therefore, I, as the Secretary of State for the Home Department, in exercise of the powers vested in me by "The Fairs Act, 1871," do hereby order that the FAIRS, which have been annually held on the 4th day of May and on Whit-Monday, in the City of Chichester, SHALL BE ABOLISHED, as from the date of this Order.

Given under my hand, at Whitehall, this 13th day of August, 1873.

(Signed)

R. LOWE.

103 *The printed poster giving notice of the abolition of the fairs held on 4 May and Whit Monday. Note the upside down 'u' in 'should' in the second paragraph!*

104 *The sole remaining part of St James's Hospital in St Pancras in an engraving of 1792, by which time it was used as a dwelling. It was founded in the 12th century as a leper house, whose inmates bathed in the River Lavant (in the foreground). St James's Fair was held in the adjacent field .*

... held in the lower part of St Pancras', which seemingly is this one: 'It was like many other small fairs those days, just to amuse children. There were all sorts of toys, gingerbread and the like. There were other amusements such as jumping in sacks, [and] donkey racing. Yes, but that fair has been done away with for many years.' If Hoare's recollections are accurate the market element of this fair had also disappeared by the early 19th century. The fair is listed by the 1889 Royal Commission, albeit moved from 25 July to 4 August, but curiously the 1871 Chichester Directory lists only three fairs – of which St James's is not one. The 1871 directory would seem to support Hoare's claim that by 1887, when he was writing, it had been 'done away with for many years'.

Michaelmas Fair

Edmund, Earl of Cornwall, claimed this fair in 1289 to take place over three days around the feast of St Michael (Michaelmas). At that time the feast of St Michael was celebrated on 10 October, but on the change from the Julian to the Gregorian calendar in 1752 it was moved to 29 September, reflecting the famous 'lost' 11 days. Despite this, the Michaelmas Fair continued to be held on 10 October, directories referring to the date as being 'Michaelmas old style'. Richard Fitzalan, who held St James's Fair, sneered at it, describing it as being 'no fair but merely a congregation of men held each year'; and then tried, unsuccessfully, to claim its profits by virtue of its being held within his Hundred.[281]

The location of this fair was quoted by George Tippen (see above) as being 'the Michaelmas Fair Field', but he gives us no directions to find it. Hoare, on the other hand, gives a description of a nameless fair, which, even if not the Michaelmas Fair itself, does give the location of its field:

> As you go from the recreation ground towards Sweepers Land, in the first field as you leave the recreation ground for many years a very large business fair used to be held. You had to go through the churchyard which was not closed as it is now, there was another way down what is called Sweepers Lane.
>
> It was a large fair for cattle, corn, cheese and hops. It was great day for country people. Now at this fair it was a rare place for the young where to buy their whips ... and new ribbons for their sweetheart's bonnets.[282]

The road along the east side of New Park recreation ground, now Alexandra Road, is shown on the 1875 Ordnance Survey map as Sweeps Lane (Hoare's Sweeper's Lane) and the churchyard Hoare refers to is the St Pancras burial ground (the Litten Ground). A study of the tithe maps of 1846-7 reveals that the Michaelmas Fair Field was a large tract of arable land running north-west from the back gardens of houses on the north side of St Pancras

105 *An extract from Loader's 1812 town plan on which the Michaelmas Fair Field has been edged in bold. The road to the north is Spitalfield Lane and the dotted line crossing the field marks the boundary between the parishes of St Pancras and St Peter the Great. Sweeps Lane can be seen running from St Pancras to the south-east corner of the site; it is now named Alexandra Road. The whole of this area has been now developed as housing.*

right through to Spitalfield Lane. The southern third of the field was in the parish of St Pancras-without-the-Walls and the remainder in St Peter the Great. In 1846 the whole field was in the occupation of Charles Farndell.

The fair Hoare describes above is a country fair of the traditional sort, with animals being traded alongside produce and fancy goods. Michaelmas Fair was not among the three listed in the 1871 Chichester Directory, suggesting that it had ceased by then, but, confusingly, it *was* noted by the aforementioned 1889 Royal Commission as still being held on 10 October. To add to the confusion, there are no fairs at all listed in the 1880 directory, even though Sloe Fair, at least, was still in operation.

In 1888 the corporation acquired three acres of the Michaelmas Fair Field fronting Spitalfield Lane to build the infectious diseases hospital, later known as the isolation hospital, and the remainder was completely built up in the 20th century to create Lewis, Turnbull and Adelaide Roads and the portion of Melbourne Road that joins them.[283] When the isolation hospital and nursing school closed they were demolished; the modern Bishopsgate Walk development now occupies the site.

Sloe Fair

The oldest of the Chichester fairs is Sloe Fair, named after the sloe tree that grew in the field outside the north gate where the fair was – and still is – held. This fair was granted by Henry I to Bishop Ralph Luffa in about 1107, to be held over eight days at a time to be selected by the bishop himself. The feast Bishop Luffa chose was that of St Faith, 6 October, but a licence of 1204 allowed this to be changed to Holy Trinity, which would have made it a moveable date between 16 May and 19 June. Dallaway, writing in 1815, gives the fair as being held on 5 October, the Eve of St Faith,

106 *Canon Gate in South Street, where the Bishop of Chichester proclaimed Sloe Fair and held his pie-powder court, until the corporation took over in 1801.*

and as the fair ran for eight days around the nominated feast it might well have commenced on the eve instead of the feast day itself.[284] Hay, however, writing in 1804, gives the date as 20 October, the date upon which the fair is now held – unless it happens to be a Sunday in which case it is translated.[285] The October dates would have put Sloe Fair within just a few days of the Michaelmas Fair.

Traditionally the Bishop of Chichester proclaimed Sloe Fair from Canon Gate, where a 'cession of authority' was formally made to him by the mayor – effectively granting him the keys of the city and the tolls during the eight-day term of his pie-powder court.[286]

In January 1801 the corporation proposed to purchase from the bishop

> the dues and tolls payable to him between the 5th and 13th October each year, and also the rights and privileges belonging to him during that period, and that £32 (being the average gross amount of such dues and market tolls for 25 years past) shall be offered as a consideration for such purchase.

This refers to Sloe Fair on its original dates, and the order for the purchase of the bishop's rights was confirmed on 12 February following.[287] From now on Sloe Fair was administered by the corporation, and the quaint episcopal proclamations and pie-powder courts ceased.

By the end of the 19th century Sloe Fair was acquiring a rather unsavoury reputation for drunkenness and immorality, and from the early 20th century it developed into the form we know today: a one-day entertainment with no market element at all.

The tolls of Sloe Fair had been collected by the corporation, but in August 1931 they decided 'by way of an experiment' to let the rights of the fair to Messrs Wall Brothers, the well-known showmen, at 10gns plus £5 for water. The experiment obviously failed, for the following February the corporation resolved to revert to the earlier arrangements, apparently with the support of the 'fair people'. The tolls charged at that time give an indication of the attractions available at Sloe Fair between the wars:[288]

Roundabouts	£1
Switchbacks	£1
Wall of Death	£1
Dodgem's (if room)	£2
Chair-O-Planes	15s.
Hoop-La's & Juvenile roundabouts	7s. 6d.
Confetti tables	2s. 6d.
Side ground per foot	2d.

The 'side ground' was presumably for stalls for selling, and the early use of the grocer's apostrophe in Dodgems and Hoop-Las will be noted.

With the onset of the Second World War in 1939 the fair was suspended for the duration, but in order to maintain the terms of the charter a token sideshow was set up each 20 October. This cessation incurred the wrath and indignation of the gossip column writer of the *Chichester Observer* when he visited Sloe Fair in 1939:

> I now add another gripe to an already long list against HITLER. When in Chichester I do not expect anything to prevent my visit to Sloe Fair and look what happened this year … I hear that one school teacher used the belief that there was a fair on to get some children to go for a walk. My, were they thrilled with the coconut shy!![289]

107 *An early 20th-century Sloe Fair which has attracted large crowds. Among the fairground rides are small stalls selling goods. Note that every head – male and female – is covered.*

108 *Sloe Fair, 1974: mud has given way to tarmac and marketing has ceased. The only trading now taking place is in hotdogs and toffee apples. Here a splendid set of gallopers plies for riders.*

The Sloe Fair field at Northgate really was a field, and as it always seemed to rain on 20 October Sloe Fair was frequently held in a sea of mud. It was a source of great delight to many generations of schoolboys (including your author) to scour the field the day after for balls lost from the coconut shies and any other interesting jetsam left behind by the showmen. This all ended in 1961 when, in conjunction with the building of the Festival Theatre on its northern boundary, the Sloe Fair field was tarmacked over to form a car park. Much of the intrinsic charm of Sloe Fair was lost, and the showmen now left nothing behind. True, it was still a fairground but hardly the 'fair ground' in which the lot fell unto the Psalmist and Rudyard Kipling!

For the young of Chichester today, Sloe Fair is one of the highlights of the year, and although it is now just a fun fair and thus a far cry from its original calling, it does constitute the sole survivor of the five ancient Chichester fairs – even if only in name.

Envoi

The 10th anniversary of the demise of the livestock market – Chichester's most famous market – was marked in October 2000 by the laying of a wreath at the site by the staff of Stride & Son and the publication in the *West Sussex Gazette* of the following sonnet, penned by Imogen Stewart, who had been Stride's livestock auctioneer's clerk:

24 October 1990
'The old order cannot hold'

Not all comprehend this is the death knell
Of the City's historic beast market;
Some take for granted the auctioneer's bell,
Whose sound rings on the air each week. And yet
this is the last time. No more pens of sheep,
Or stores, no cull cows, no fattened cattle;
The once busy market place falls asleep
No more woken by auctioneers' patter.
Outside, the beasts patiently wait their doom,
Inside, a general expression of gloom;
Around the ring farmers silently mourn
Part of their lives since before they were born,
Market history encircles Cicestrian lives:
Now the farmers' market our tradition revives.

Market history does indeed encircle Cicestrians' lives – the Market Cross sees to that – but as the corn market closed in 1975, followed by the livestock market in 1990 and the daily covered market in 2009, the question has to be asked whether Chichester can still be considered a market town in the strictest sense of the word. A natural first reaction might be that it is no longer so.

However, when the selling of livestock ceased over 20 years ago, general market trading continued in the newly created car park that still bears the

109   A bustling farmers' market in East Street, August 2011. The stalls are provided by Chichester District Council.

110   The last continental Christmas market, held on Sunday 28 November 2010 in the Friary Lane car park.

name Cattle Market. Every Wednesday and Saturday traders set up their stalls dealing in fruit, vegetables, fish, household goods, garden plants, shoes and clothing. There is even an extra market on each Bank Holiday Monday, which is accompanied by a car boot sale.

The farmers' market, to which the poet refers in her sonnet, was introduced by Chichester District Council in 1998 as part of a popular national initiative to enable farmers and growers to sell direct to the public, cutting out the middle-man. Those trading at the market are required to sell only their own wares, which must have been grown, reared, baked or preserved within 30 miles of Chichester. Chichester's Farmers' Market, held on the first and third Fridays of the month, started out life on the Cattle Market site but suffered from the problem that few knew it was there. It was moved into the city centre, therefore, its stalls in North and East Streets providing a revival of the street markets that had ceased in 1808 when the Market House opened; a revival that was to prove slightly ironic because in 2009 the Market House (a.k.a. the Butter Market) ceased to be a market – so a reversal of history had been brought about. The re-sited farmers' market now adds a welcome, twice-monthly touch of almost continental colour to the Chichester street scene.

On the matter of continental colour, the city council introduced annual Christmas markets in 2000, held on a Sunday in November. Traders, mostly from France, would set up stalls offering a tempting variety of goods and foodstuffs that were otherwise not easily available in Chichester. Alas, these markets often seemed to attract bad weather and hence drew disappointing attendances, so that of 2010 proved to be the last, and it was replaced by an indoor Christmas market in 2011.

So is Chichester still a market town? As there are still regular traders' and farmers' markets the answer has to be yes. However, although one of those traders' markets is held on a Wednesday, Wednesday is no longer market day in the way it was up to the 1960s when it was something of a day out – people would flock into the city from the outlying farms and villages, many brought in by Southdown's 'Wednesdays only' bus services; the stentorian tones of Stride's and Wyatt's auctioneers would ring out over the squeal of pigs and the confused bleating of Southdown sheep; farmers' wives would shop and the pubs would be heaving at lunchtime – with attendant bacchanalian behaviour. Those days, like 'Darling Clementine', are lost and gone forever.

111 *The Chichester Cattle Market bell, now living in retirement in Stride & Son's auction rooms. The bell is dated 1897 and thus post-dates the Cattle Market by 26 years, so it was probably supplied by Charles Stride for his own use.*

References

1. James Dallaway, *A History of the Western Division of the County of Sussex*, 1815
2. I am indebted to Dr David Pilbeam of the Faculty of Biological Sciences, University of Leeds, for providing me with this information.
3. Roy Morgan, *Chichester, a Documentary History*, Phillimore, 1992
4. Alexander Hay, *The History of Chichester interspersed with various Notes and Observations on the Early and Present State of the City*, Seagrave, 1804
5. Pilbeam, *op. cit.*
6. WSRO John Marsh, *Journal of my private life*, available on microfilm, the originals being in America
7. Michael Holland (ed.), *Swing Unmasked*, FACHRS Publications, 2005
8. John Lowerson, *A Short History of Sussex*, William Dawson and Son, 1980
9. Christopher Morris (ed.), *William Cobbett's Illustrated Rural Rides*, Webb & Bowers, 1984
10. Mike Matthews, *Captain Swing in Sussex and Kent – Rural rebellion in 1830*, Hastings Press, 2006
11. WSRO AddMS 5293 Chichester Corn Exchange Co. Shareholders' Minute Book 1832-1905 records throughput of corn at the Corn Exchange
12. R.H.B. Jesse, *A Survey of the Agriculture of Sussex*, Royal Agricultural Society, 1960
13. H. Rider Haggard, *Rural England; Being an account of agricultural and social researches carried out in the years 1901 &1902*, vol. 1, Longmans, Green and Co., 1906
14. A.D. Hall and E.J. Russell, *A Report on the Agriculture and Soils of Kent, Surrey and Sussex*, HMSO, 1911
15. *Agriculture in Sussex 1948* contains an article by R.H.B. Jesse on this subject. County Associates Ltd.
16. R. Thurston Hopkins, *Kipling's Sussex Revisited*, 1929
17. H. George Hughs, 'The History of Southdown Sheep', Southdown Sheep Society website
18. *General View of the Agriculture of the County of Sussex*, 1808
19. Chichester Directories.
20. *Chichester Review* August 1947 carried a report of the show.
21. WSRO MF 625-56, microfilms of land tax records for West Sussex parishes, 1780-1832
22. WSRO MP19 William Hoare, *An account of conversations which took place between Old Age and William Young commencing on 21 April 1887 concerning the changes Old Age has seen and can remember that has taken place in the City of Chichester within the last 70 years.* Hoare was only semi-literate and this memoir was written in the form of a conversation with his younger self. MP 19 is a typewritten transcription of Hoare's text but retains the rather quaint misspellings and malapropisms. It provides accounts of many features of Chichester in the early 19th century.
23. *Chichester Observer*, 30 September 1936
24. *Victoria County History: Sussex*, 1935, p.97
25. Hay, *op. cit.*, gives a translation of the 1685 Charter, the original of which – in Latin – is at WSRO. Seagrave, 1804.
26. WSRO Chichester City archive AZ/2 the 'Brown Book', which contains a transcription of the charter in Latin with a translation into English alongside.
27. Samuel & Nathaniel Buck, *The South-West Prospect of the City of Chichester*, 1738. The Buck brothers produced panoramic views of most of the principal towns and cities in England and Wales in the early 18th century, and each carried a description of the place and its trade.
28. Hay, *op. cit.*
29. WSRO C/1 Chichester Common Council minute book, 1685-1737, and C/3 Chichester Common Council minute book, 1783-1826.
30. Paul Foster (ed.), *A Jewel in Stone, Chichester Market Cross 1501-2001*, Otter Memorial Paper 15, University College, Chichester
31. Hay, *op. cit.*
32. P. Holland (trans.), *Britain*, contains this description by Camden, which was published in 1610
33. Francis Steer (ed.), *The Memoirs of James Spershott*, edited from the manuscript at WSRO (Add MS 2791) and published in 1962 as Chichester Paper no. 30 (CP 30), Chichester City Council
34. WSRO C/1, *op. cit.*
35. Alan H.J. Green, *The Building of Georgian Chichester*, gives a full account of the building of the new Council House. Phillimore, 2007.
36. CP30, *op. cit.*
37. WSRO C/1, *op. cit.*
38. WSRO C/3, *op. cit.*

39. WSRO C/2, Chichester Common Council minute book, 1738-83
40. WSRO C/3, *op. cit.*
41. Green, *op. cit.*
42. CP30, *op. cit.*
43. Hay, *op. cit.*
44. Hay, *op. cit.*
45. WSRO C/1 Chichester Common Council minute book, 1685-1737
46. WSRO MP19 Hoare, *op. cit.*
47. WSRO C/2 Chichester Common Council minute book, 1738-83
48. WSRO Chichester City Archive AL/108, the lease from the Mayor and Corporation to James Beeding, 3 April 1767. It refers to the piece of ground as formerly being called 'the pound'.
49. Alison McCann, *The history of the Church and Parish of St Andrew Oxmarket, Chichester,* WSRO 1978
50. WSRO C/3 Chichester Common Council minute book, 1783-1826
51. *Ibid.*
52. *Ibid.*
53. 47 GeoIII Cap 84. Royal Assent was granted on 8 August 1807.
54. Alan H.J. Green, *St John's Chapel and the New Town, Chichester,* Phillimore, 2005
55. WSRO C/3, *op. cit.*
56. WSRO Par42/13/4, a handwritten agreement signed by six of the proprietors of Newtown
57. WSRO C/5 Chichester Common Council minute book, 1835-40
58. WSRO C/6 Chichester Common Council minute book, 1840-4
59. *Ibid.*
60. WSRO C/7 City Council minute book, 1845-51
61. WSRO C/8 City Council minute book, 1851-8
62. WSRO C/9 City Council minute book, 1858-64
63. Alan H.J. Green, 'Halsted & Sons of Chichester, Engineers and Ironfounders', *Sussex Industrial History* no. 35, Sussex Industrial Archaeology Society, 2005
64. WSRO C/9, *op. cit.*
65. WSRO C/10 City Council minute book, 1864-8
66. WSRO C/11 City Council minute book, 1868-71
67. *West Sussex Gazette,* 27 April 1871
68. *West Sussex Gazette,* 4 May 1871.
69. WSRO C/3 Chichester Common Council minute book, 1783-1826
70. *Ibid.*
71. 47 GeoIII Cap 84.
72. WSRO C/3, *op. cit.*
73. WSRO, *ibid.*
74. Francis Steer, CP27 *The Market House, Chichester,* Chichester City Council, 1962
75. WSRO C/3, *op. cit.*
76. Dallaway, James, *A History of the Western Division of the County of Sussex,* 1815
77. *Ibid.*
78. WSRO C/4 Chichester Common Council minute book, 1827-35
79. WSRO CA/1 and onwards, Chichester Council Committee minute books into which the proceedings of all the various committees are recorded. The Market House was initially run by the Parliamentary, Railway and General Purposes Committee.
80. WSRO C/5 Chichester Common Council minute book, 1835-40
81. WSRO C/8 Chichester Council minute book, 1851-8
82. WSRO C/9 Chichester Council minute book, 1858-64
83. WSRO C/13 Chichester Council minute book, 1875-8
84. WSRO CA/3 Chichester Council Committee minute book, 1879-84
85. WSRO CA/7 and CA/8 Chichester Council Committee minute books, 1892-4 and 1894-6.
86. WSRO C/16 Chichester Council minute book, 1885-8
87. WSRO J/8, a bundle of printed copies of various Chichester bylaws
88. WSRO C/19 Chichester Council minute book, 1896-9
89. WSRO C/21 Chichester Council minute book, 1899-1902
90. WSRO CA/10 Chichester Council Committee minute book, 1898-1900
91. WSRO CA/11 Chichester Council Committee minute book, 1900-2
92. WSRO CA/12 Chichester Council Committee minute book, 1902-4
93. WSRO CA/17 to 20 Chichester Council Committee minute books, 1904-27
94. WSRO CA/21& 22 Chichester Council Committee minute books, 1927-30
95. Tony Catton, *In and around Chichester,* published privately in 1942 by Charles J. Kimbell, Wellington, NSW, Australia
96. WSRO CA/26 Chichester Council Committee minute book, 1935-6
97. WSRO CD/1 Chichester Council Finance Committee minute book, 1936-49 and CAA/1 Markets Committee minute book, 1949-66
98. *Chichester Observer,* 29 January 1949, a public notice about the corporation's application for a Provisional Order and the date and time of the public inquiry
99. *Chichester Observer,* 12 February 1949
100. 12 & 13 Geo 6 Ch. xxiv Ministry of Health Provisional Order Confirmation (Chichester) Act 1949
101. WSRO CAA/1, *op. cit.*
102. WSRO CD/2 Chichester Council Finance Committee minute book, 1949-58
103. WSRO CAA/1, *op. cit.*
104. *Ibid.*
105. *Ibid.*
106. WSRO CE/2 Chichester City Council, Cemetery, Parks & Allotments Committee minute book, 1958-74.
107. *Ibid.*
108. Chichester District Council, planning application 07/02223/LBC, 2 May 2007. The Design and Access Statement describes the underlying principles behind the proposals.
109. *Ibid.*, letter of withdrawal
110. Chichester District Council, planning application 07/04980/LBC, dated 4 October 2007
111. Rodney Duggua, 'The Buttermarket: the Phoenix Rises', *Chichester Society Newsletter,* no. 168, March 2011. Duggua, the town clerk, submitted the article on behalf of Chichester City Council.
112. www.chichester.co.uk/blog (no longer accessible)
113. *Chichester Observer,* 16 August 2008 and Duggua, *op. cit.*
114. Chichester District Council, planning application 08/05203, 24 December 2008
115. WSRO CA/1 Chichester Council Committee Meeting minute book, 1867-73
116. WSRO C/13 Chichester Common Council minute book, 1875-8
117. WSRO C/14 Chichester Common Council minute book, 1879-81
118. Francis Steer, CP27, *op. cit.*
119. WSRO C/4 Chichester Common Council minute book, 1827-35
120. John Summerson, *Georgian London,* Barrie & Jenkins, 1988
121. James Elmes, *A Topographical Dictionary of London and its Environs,* 1831

122. Howard Colvin, *A Biographical Dictionary of British Architects 1600-1840*, John Murray, 1978
123. Tolls quoted in 'The Rules of The Corn Exchange, Chichester' (in the author's collection).
124. WSRO AddMS 5293 Chichester Corn Exchange Minute Book, 1832-1905
125. *Hampshire Telegraph*, 21 May 1832, carried a notice about the forthcoming sale
126. West Sussex Library Service S157392, a copy of the printed rules
127. *Hampshire Telegraph*, 16 July 1832
128. Colvin, *op. cit.*
129. Nikolaus Pevsner and Ian Nairn, *The Buildings of England – Sussex*, Penguin, 1965
130. Letter from Howard Colvin to the author
131. *Hampshire Telegraph*, 17 December 1832
132. Alison Kelly, *Mrs Coade's Stone*, self-published 1990, lists the contents of the firm's order books
133. *Hampshire Telegraph*, 11 February 1833
134. WSRO AddMS 5293, *op. cit.*
135. WSRO MP 2326, 30 Southgate, and AddMS 36001-9, deeds to 30 Southgate
136. Colvin, *op. cit.*
137. WSRO Chichester City C/5 Common Council minute book, 1835-40
138. WSRO Chichester City E/3, Paving Commissioners' minute book, 1825-45
139. WSRO AddMS 5293 Shareholders' minute book, 1832-1905
140. Matthew 13 vv 24-30.
141. The *London Gazette* of 22 May 1877 carried a notice about his demise and the sale of his estate, which included five shares in the Chichester Corn Exchange
142. WSRO AddMS 5293, *op. cit.*
143. WSRO Raper 43, copies of the sale particulars, one of which has been marked up with the purchasers and the prices paid
144. WSRO AddMS 5293, *op. cit.*
145. WSRO AddMS 6155, indenture conveying the site upon which 19 and 20 St John's Street were to be built refers to the vacant plots to the south in its abuttals
146. WSRO AddMS 2730, memo book of C.T. Halsted, records completion of the order for the columns
147. WSRO AddMS 5294, Corn Exchange Company committee minute book 1877-1905
148. *Ibid.*
149. *Ibid.*
150. *Ibid.*
151. Information supplied to the author by Ann Griffiths (*née* Freeland), a descendant of the Raper and Freeland families
152. WSRO AddMS 5293, *op. cit.*
153. WSRO AddMS 5295, Corn Exchange Company Directors' minute book, 1905-19
154. WSRO Raper uncatalogued, Acc 7820, Box 1, Corn Exchange Shareholders' minute book, 1905-47
155. *Ibid.*
156. WSRO AddMS 5295, *op. cit.*
157. WSRO Add MS 14393, a collection of printed annual reports of the Corn Exchange Company
158. *Agriculture in Sussex 1948* – contains an article by R.H.B. Jesse, County Associates Ltd
159. WSRO AddMS 5296 Corn Exchange Company Directors' minute book, 1919-33
160. *Chichester Observer*, 23 November 1927
161. WSRO AddMS 5296, *op. cit.*
162. *Ibid.*
163. WSRO AddMS 5297, Chichester Corn Exchange Co. cash book, 1914-41
164. *Ibid.*
165. WSRO AddMS 5296, *op. cit.*
166. WSRO AddMS 5298 Chichester Corn Exchange Co. dividend book, 1915-22, and AddMS 5299, Chichester Corn Exchange Co. dividend book, 1923-36
167. WSRO Raper uncatalogued Acc 7820, Box 1, Chichester Corn Exchange shareholders' minute book, 1905-47
168. As remembered by the late Mrs Kathleen Stephens and retold to the author
169. WSRO CG/1, Chichester City Council Highway Committee minute book, 1936-50
170. WSRO Raper uncatalogued Acc 7820 Box 2, a bundle of printed notices of annual general meetings, 1942-6
171. WSRO Raper uncatalogued Acc 7820 Box 1, shareholders' minute book, *op. cit.*
172. *Ibid.*, shareholders' minute book, *op. cit.*
173. *Ibid.*, spreadsheet of accounts 1 May 1946 to 12 March 1947 includes this figure
174. Copy of the typed liquidator's report, Pat Combes collection
175. WSRO CAA/1 Chichester Council Markets Committee minute book, 1949-66
176. Land Registry search of the Chichester Corn Exchange deeds
177. Information given in an undated (1930s) letter to the young David Sadler from his aunt
178. *London Gazette*, 22 May 1877, public notice about the disposal of Henry Sadler's estate pursuant to a High Court Order
179. WSRO AddMS 5295, Chichester Corn Exchange, directors' minute book, 1905-19
180. Chichester Directories 1880-7 list the businesses at 40 East Street
181. WSRO AddMS 14345, Wyatt & Co., valuer's notebook, entry made on 28 December 1898
182. The Chichester Directory of 1895 lists Mrs Sadler as living at their Oving Road house, suggesting she had been widowed, but the business is still listed as Robert Sadler. Subsequent directories give the changed identities of the company.
183. Invoice from Arnold, Cooper & Tomkins to Frederick Sadler for legal fees in connection with the transfer of title, August to October 1905. David Sadler collection.
184. Rita Blakenry, *Fishbourne, A village history*, self-published 1984, r/p 2007
185. Land Registry search, *op. cit.*
186. The letter sent to D. Combes, Pat Combes collection.
187. Francis W. Steer, 'The *Dolphin & Anchor Hotel*, Chichester', Chichester Paper no. 23 (CP23), Chichester City Council, 1961
188. WSRO AddMS 5293 Chichester Corn Exchange shareholders' minute book, 1832-1905
189. WSRO AddMS29707 a reprinted article from the *West Sussex Gazette* of 11 May 1937 entitled 'Memories of West Wittering – Mr C.C. Combes looks back'
190. WSRO AddMS 5295 and Raper uncatalogued Acc 7820 Box 2, *op. cit.*

191. Told to the author by Pat Combes
192. WSRO Raper uncatalogued Acc 7820 Box 2, *op. cit.*
193. Copy of the letter in the Pat Combes collection
194. Pat Combes, unpublished paper giving the history of the New Corn Exchange venture
195. WSRO C/11 Common Council minute book, 1868-71
196. *West Sussex Gazette*, 11 May 1871. Its report on the opening of the New Cattle Market gave the full story of the battle of the sites with much more information than is contained in the minute books.
197. WSRO C/11, *op. cit.*
198. *Ibid.*
199. *Ibid.*
200. 31 & 32 Vict. – Ch. Lxvii
201. Alan H.J. Green, 'Halsted & Sons of Chichester' in *Sussex Industrial History* no. 35, Sussex Industrial Archaeology Society, 2005
202. *West Sussex Gazette*, 14 April 1870, carried a lengthy – and glowing – report of the proceedings
203. WSRO C/11, *op. cit.*
204. *Ibid.*
205. *West Sussex Gazette*, 11 May 1871
206. *West Sussex Gazette*, 18 May 1871. It carried a full report of the dinner, which was not able to be included in the previous week's issue owing to reporting deadlines.
207. *West Sussex Gazette*, 11 May 1871
208. WSRO C/11 *op. cit.*
209. WSRO C/21 Common Council minute book 1871-5
210. *Ibid.*
211. *Hampshire Telegraph*, 4 January and 4 March 1882
212. WSRO CA/4 Chichester Council Committee meeting book, 1884-8
213. WSRO CA/2 Chichester Council Committee meeting book, 1873-9
214. *Ibid.*
215. WSRO CA/3 Chichester Council Committee meeting book, 1879-84
216. WSRO CA/5 Chichester Council Committee meeting book, 1888-90
217. *Ibid.*
218. WSRO CA/6 Chichester Council Committee meeting book, 1890-2
219. WSRO CA/7 Chichester Council Committee meeting book, 1892-4
220. WSRO CA/8 Chichester Council Committee meeting book, 1894-6
221. WSRO CA/10 Chichester Council Committee meeting book, 1898-1900
222. WSRO Chichester Council Committee meeting books; CA/11 1900-2, and CA/12 1902-4
223. H. Rider Haggard, *Rural England; Being an account of agricultural and social researches carried out in the years 1901 &1902*, vol. 1, Longmans, Green and Co., 1906
224. WSRO CA/12, *op. cit.*
225. WSRO Chichester Council Committee meeting books; CA/12, *op. cit.* and CA/13 1904-7
226. WSRO CA/13, *op. cit.*
227. WSRO CA/14 Chichester Council Committee meeting book 1907-10
228. WSRO CA/15 Chichester Council Committee meeting book, 1910-13
229. WSRO CA/16 Chichester Council Committee meeting book, 1913-16
230. Dan Stride, *The Stride Family 1700-2000,* privately published, second edn November 2000
231. *Ibid.*
232. WSRO CA/17 Chichester Council Committee meeting book, 1916-20
233. WSRO CA/18 Chichester Council Committee meeting book, 1920-2
234. *Chichester Observer*, 22 October 1976, 'Wyatt and Son celebrates 150 Years'
235. WSRO CA/18, *op. cit.*
236. WSRO CA/19 and CA/20 Chichester Council Committee meeting books, 1922-5 and 1925-7
237. WSRO CA/20, *op. cit.*
238. WSRO CA/23 and CA/25 Chichester Council Committee meeting books, 1930-2 and 1934-5
239. WSRO CG/1 Chichester Council Highways Committee minute book, 1936-50
240. Dan Stride, *op. cit.*
241. Ken Green, 'The day the Liberator bomber crashed on Chichester', New Chichester Paper No. 1, Chichester Local History Society, and the University of Chichester, 2010
242. WSRO CG/1, *op. cit.*
243. Published by the Southern Publishing Co. Ltd for Chichester Corporation in February 1949
244. WSRO CG/1, *op. cit.*
245. WSRO CAA/1 Chichester City Council Special (Cattle Market) Committee minute book 1949-66
246. Chichester Corporation, Abstract of Accounts for the year ended 31 March 1949
247. Dan Stride, *op. cit.*
248. WSRO CAA/1 *op. cit.*
249. WSRO CG/2 Chichester Council Highways Committee minute book, 1950-68
250. WSRO Cutten D1/1/6 John D. Willis, 'Chichester Market 1950-1990', photocopy of a printed article n/d from an unidentified publication
251. WSRO CAA/1, *op. cit.*
252. *Ibid.*
253. WSRO CG/1, *op. cit.*
254. WSRO CAA/1, *op. cit.*
255. WSRO Cutten D1/1/6, *op. cit.*
256. WSRO CAA/1, *op. cit.*
257. WSRO CE/2 Chichester Council Markets, Cemetery, Parks and Allotments Committee minute book, 1958-74
258. WSRO DC/CH/3/11/1 Chichester District Council Public Services Committee minute book, 1973-6
259. WSRO DC/CH/3/11/2 Chichester District Council Public Services Committee minute book, 1976-8
260. As told to the author by Derek Bowerman.
261. WSRO DC/CH/3/11/1 to 3 incl. Chichester District Council Public Services Committee minute books, 1973-80
262. WSRO DC/CH/3/11/4 Chichester District Council Public Services Committee minute book, 1980-3
263. WSRO DC/CH/3/11/4 to 5 incl. Chichester District Council Public Services Committee minute books, 1980-5
264. 'Chichester Market – An illustrated commentary on the past, present and future of the livestock and retail markets', complied, written and published by the Chichester Society, 1986.
265. WSRO DC/CH/1/1/5 Chichester District Council minutes, 1988-91
266. WSRO DC/CH/3/1/9 Chichester District Council Policy and

Resources Committee minutes, 1989-90

267. WSRO DC/CH/1/1/5, *op. cit.*

268. WSRO DC/CH/3/1/10 Chichester District Council Policy and Resources Committee minutes, 1990-1

269. James Dallaway, *A History of the Western Division of the County of Sussex*, 1815, offers these derivations

270. Benjamin Martin, *The Natural History of England*, 1759. Martin was an instrument maker who lived in Chichester from the late 1720s to 1742.

271. *Victoria County History: Sussex*, 1935, p.98 quotes the Royal Commission

272. WSRO A/7 Chichester City Archive, a transcription of the 1500 charter

273. WSRO AZ/2 Chichester City Archives, transcriptions of the city charters. It does not include that of 1685 (the original is missing) but a full transcription of it is given by Alexander Hay *(see ref 4)*

274. WSRO AZ/5 Chichester City Archive, papers relating to the abolition of fairs held on 4 May and Whit Monday 1873

275. WSRO MP19 Hoare, *op. cit.*

276. T.G. Willis, *Records of Chichester – some glimpses of its past*, 1928. Willis gives a transcript of Tippen's 'Recollections of Chichester from 1840 to 1925'.

277. WSRO AZ/5, *op. cit.*

278. *Ibid.*, item 10 in the bundle of documents is a printed pro-forma in which the Town Council of Chichester has been entered against 'Lords or Owners'.

279. *Ibid.*, the draft notice states that the Whit Monday Fair was held in the streets.

280. VCH, *op. cit.*, p.98

281. *Ibid.*

282. WSRO MP 19, *op. cit.*

283. WSRO CA/4 Chichester Council Committee minute book 1884-8 refers to the building of the Infectious Diseases Hospital on the Michaelmas Fair Field

284. Dallaway, *op. cit.*

285. Hay, Alexander, *op. cit.*

286. *Ibid.*

287. WSRO C/3 Chichester Common Council minute book, 1783-1836. Dallaway (*op. cit.*), however, says that the transfer took place in 1807 rather than 1801.

288. WSRO CA/23 Chichester City Council committee minute book, 1930-2

289. *Chichester Observer*, 28 October 1939. The gossip column was called 'Whispered Confidences'.

Index

Figures in **bold** refer to illustration numbers.